RESTRICTED AN 01-190FB-1

GRUMMAN F4F (FM-2) WILDCAT
Pilot's Flight Operating Instructions

THIS PUBLICATION SUPERSEDES AN 01-190F-1
DATED 1 APRIL 1944 REVISED 5 AUGUST 1944

This manual is sold for historic research purposes only, as an entertainment. It is not intended to be used as part of an actual flight training program. No book can substitute for flight training by an authorized instructor. The licensing of pilots is overseen by organizations and authorities such as the FAA and CAA. Operating an aircraft without the proper license is a federal crime.

©2006-2010 Periscope Film LLC
All Rights Reserved
ISBN #978-1-935327-98-1
www.PeriscopeFilm.com

RESTRICTED AN 01-190FB-1

Pilot's Handbook
of
Flight Operating Instructions

NAVY MODEL

FM-2 Airplane

THIS PUBLICATION SUPERSEDES AN 01-190F-1
DATED 1 APRIL 1944 REVISED 5 AUGUST 1944

Appendix I of this publication shall not be carried in aircraft on combat missions or when there is a reasonable chance of its falling into the hands of the enemy

NOTICE.—This document contains information affecting the national defense of the United States within the meaning of the Espionage Act, 50 U. S. C., 31 and 32, as amended. Its transmission or the revelation of its contents in any manner to an unauthorized person is prohibited by law.

15 February 1945

RESTRICTED

Published under joint authority of the Commanding General, Army Air Forces, the Chief of the Bureau of Aeronautics, and the Air Council of the United Kingdom

THIS PUBLICATION MAY BE USED BY PERSONNEL RENDERING SERVICE TO THE UNITED STATES OR ITS ALLIES

Navy Regulations, Article 76, contains the following statements relating to the handling of restricted matter:

Par. (9) (*a*). Restricted matter may be disclosed to persons of the Military or Naval Establishments in accordance with special instructions issued by the originator or other competent authority, or in the absence of special instructions, as determined by the local administrative head charged with custody of the subject matter.

(*b*) Restricted matter may be disclosed to persons of discretion in the Government service when it appears to be in the public interest.

(*c*) Restricted matter may be disclosed, under special circumstances, to persons not in the Government service when it appears to be in the public interest.

The Bureau of Aeronautics Aviation Circular Letter No. 31–44 contains the following paragraph relative to the use of technical aeronautics publications:

Par. 8. *Distribution to All Interested Personnel.*—In connection with the distribution of aeronautical publications within any activity, it should be borne in mind by the officers responsible for such distribution that technical publications are issued specifically for use not only by officer personnel, but more particularly by responsible civilian and enlisted personnel working with or servicing equipment to which the information applies.

Paragraph 5 (*d*) of Army Regulation 380–5 relative to the handling of restricted printed matter is quoted below:

(*d*) *Dissemination of restricted matter.*—The information contained in restricted documents and the essential characteristics of restricted material may be given to any person known to be in the service of the United States and to persons of undoubted loyalty and discretion who are cooperating in Government work, but will not be communicated to the public or to the press except by authorized military public relations agencies.

These instructions permit the issue of restricted publications to civilian contract and other accredited schools engaged in training personnel for Government work, to civilian concerns contracting for overhaul and repair of aircraft or aircraft accessories and to similar commercial organizations.

---— LIST OF REVISED PAGES ISSUED ---—

NOTE.—A heavy black vertical line to the left of the text on revised pages indicates the extent of the revision. This line is omitted where more than 50 percent of the page is involved.

ADDITIONAL COPIES OF THIS PUBLICATION MAY BE OBTAINED AS FOLLOWS:

AAF ACTIVITIES.—Submit requisitions to the Commanding General, Fairfield Air Service Command, Patterson Field, Fairfield, Ohio, Attention: Publications Distribution Branch, in accordance with AAF Regulation No. 5–9. Also, for details of Technical Order distribution, see T. O. No. 00–25–3.

NAVY ACTIVITIES.—Submit requests to Chief, BuAer, Navy Department, Washington, D. C., Attn.: Publications Section on order form NAVAER–140. For complete listing of available material and details of distribution see Naval Aeronautic Publications Index, NavAer 00–500.

RESTRICTED

RESTRICTED
AN 01-190FB-1

TABLE OF CONTENTS

SECTION I
DESCRIPTION

1. General Description 1
2. Surface Controls 1
3. Tab Controls 3
   a. Aileron Tab 3
   b. Elevator Tabs 3
   c. Rudder Tab 3
4. Wing Flap System 3
5. Power Plant Controls 4
   a. Throttle and Mixture Controls 4
   b. Supercharger Control 4
   c. Propeller Control 5
   d. Carburetor Air Control 5
   e. Cowl Flap Control and Cylinder Head Temperatures 6
   f. Ignition Switch 6
   g. Priming System and Control 6
   h. Starter and Control 6
6. Fuel System 11
   a. Description 11
   b. Tank Selector Valve 11
   c. Electric Emergency Fuel Pump 11
   d. Fuel Quantity Gauge 13
   e. Low Fuel Warning Light 13
   f. Droppable Fuel Tank Release 13
   g. Vapor Return 13
7. Oil System 13
   a. Description 13
   b. Oil Dilution System 13
8. Anti-Detonant Injection System 13
9. Landing Gear Controls 15
   a. Retracting Mechanism 15
   b. Handcrank Brake 15
   c. Position of Wheels 15
   d. Extended Position Lock 15
   e. Brake Control 15
   f. Arresting Hook Control 15
   g. Tail Wheel Caster Lock 16
10. Wing Folding 16
    a. Controls 16
    b. Safety Indicator 16
    c. To Fold Wings 16
    d. To Spread Wings 16
11. Armament Controls 17
    a. Gunnery Controls 17
       (1) General Description 17
       (2) Gun Charging 17
       (3) Gun Firing 17
       (4) Gun Sights 17
       (5) Gun Camera 18
       (6) Electrical Gun Heaters 18
    b. Rocket Installation 18
    c. Tow Target 18
    d. Pyrotechnics 18
12. Electrical System 18
    a. General Description 18
    b. Electrical Controls 18a
    c. Cockpit Lighting 18a
    d. Special Lighting 18a

13. Auxiliary Controls 19
    a. Sliding Canopy 19
       (1) Operation 19
       (2) Emergency Release 19
    b. Windshield Defroster 19
    c. Cockpit Air Intake 19
    d. Pilot's Seat Adjustment 19
    e. Shoulder Harness 19
    f. Map Case 20
    g. Chart Board 20

SECTION II
PILOT OPERATING INSTRUCTIONS

1. Before Entering the Pilot's Compartment 21
   a. Flight Limitations and Restrictions 21
      (1) Maneuvers Prohibited 21
      (2) Permissible Accelerations 21
      (3) Limiting Airspeeds 21
   b. Effect of Initial Gross Weight 21
   c. Airplane Entry 21
2. Pre-Flight Check Lists 21
   a. Pilot's Standard Check List 21
   b. Special Night Check List 23
3. Fuel System Management 23
4. Function of the Manifold Pressure Regulator 23
5. War Emergency Power 23
6. Starting 24
   a. Normal Starting Check-off List 24
   b. Hard Starting 25
   c. Emergency Operation of Cartridge Starters 26
   d. In Case of Fire 26
7. Ground Check 26
   a. Warm-Up 26
   b. Engine Check 27
   c. Magneto Check 27
   d. Carburetor Idle Mixture Check 27
   e. Manifold Pressure Regulator Check 28
   f. Propeller Operation Check 28
   g. Supercharger Desludging Operation 29
   h. Supercharger Check 29
8. Emergency Take-Off 29
9. Taxiing Instructions 32
10. Take-Off 32
    a. Discussion 32
    b. Expanded Take-Off Check List 32
11. Engine Failure During Take-Off 32
12. Climb 32
    a. Discussion 32
    b. Rated Power Climb 32
    c. Military Power Climb 33
    d. War Emergency Power Climb 33
13. General Flying Characteristics 33
    a. Cruising Below Normal Rated Power 33
    b. Changing Power Conditions 33
    c. Supercharger Operation 33
    d. Stability 34
    e. Maneuvers with ADI 34
    f. Operation of ADI System for Familiarization 35

RESTRICTED

i

		Page
14.	Stalls	35
15.	Spins	36
16.	Acrobatics	36
17.	Diving	36
	a. Discussion	36
	b. Expanded Diving Check-Off List	36
18.	Night Flying	37
19.	Approach and Landing	37
	a. Expanded Landing Check-Off List	37
	b. Cross Wind Landing	37
	c. Wave-Off Condition List	37
20.	Stopping the Engine	37
	a. Expanded Pilot's Check-Off List	37
	b. Oil Dilution Procedure	37
21.	Tying Down	39
	a. Parking Harness	39
	b. Mooring	41

SECTION III
OPERATING DATA

1.	Power Plant Chart	43
2.	Air Speed Correction Table	43

SECTION IV
EMERGENCY OPERATING INSTRUCTIONS

1.	Sliding Canopy Emergency Release	44
2.	Fires	
	a. Engine Fires	44
	b. Wing Fires	44
3.	Engine Failure	45
4.	Wheels Up Landing	45
5.	Water Landing — Ditching	45
6.	Generator Failure	45
7.	MP Regulator Failure	45

SECTION V
OPERATIONAL EQUIPMENT

1.	Oxygen System	47
	a. Description	47
	b. Operation	47
	(1) General	47
	(2) When to Use Oxygen	47
	c. Preflight Check	47
	d. Recharging Cylinder	48
	e. Man-Hour Oxygen Consumption Table	48

2.	Operation of Radio Equipment	48
	a. Description	48
	(1) General	48
	(2) Airplanes Serial No. 15952 - 46942 incl.	49
	(3) Airplanes Serial No. 46943 - 57043 incl.	49
	(4) Airplanes Serial No. 57044 and Subsequent	49
	b. Operation of Communication Equipment	49
	(1) GF-12/RU-17 Communication Equipment	49
	(a) To Receive	49
	(b) To Transmit Voice	49
	(c) To Transmit in Code	49
	(2) AN/ARC-4 Communication Equipment	49
	(a) To Receive	49
	(b) To Transmit	53
	(3) AN/ARC-1 Communication Equipment	53
	(a) To Receive	53
	(b) To Transmit	53
	c. Operation of Navigation Equipment	53
	(1) ZB-3 Navigation Equipment	53
	(2) AN/ARR-2 Navigation Equipment	53
	(3) AN/ARR-2a Navigation Equipment	53
	(4) BC1206 Range Receiver	53
	d. Simultaneous Reception of Navigation and Communication Equipment	54
	(1) GF-12/RU-17 Communication Equipment and ZB-3 Navigation Equipment	54
	(2) AN/ARC-4 Communication Equipment and AN/ARR-2 Navigation Equipment	54
	(3) AN/ARC-1 Communication Equipment and AN/ARR-2a Navigation Equipment	54
	e. Pre-Flight Radio Test	54

SECTION VI
EXTREME WEATHER OPERATION

1.	General Discussion	55
2.	Arctic and Cold Weather Operation	55
	a. Windshield Defroster	55
	b. Oil Dilution	55
	c. Pilot Tube Heater	55
	d. Electric Gun Heaters	55
3.	Desert and Extreme Dry and Dusty Climate Operation	55
4.	Tropic and Extreme Hot Weather Operation	55

APPENDIX I

Personnel Protection Against Gunfire	58
Take-Off, Climb and Landing Chart	59
Flight Operation Instruction Chart	60
Angle of Attack vs. Indicated Airspeed	62
Engine Calibration Curve	63

RESTRICTED
AN 01-190FB-1

ILLUSTRATION LIST

FIG. NO.	TITLE	PAGE NO.
1.	Airplane Access	iv
2.	Pedal Adjustment Procedure	1
3.	Wing Flap Operation	2
4.	Tab Controls	3
5.	Instrument Panel	7
6.	Left Hand Side of Cockpit	8
7.	Right Hand Side of Cockpit	9
8.	Fuel System Diagram	10
9.	Oil System Diagram	12
10.	ADI System Diagram	14
11.	Arresting Hook Operation	16
12.	Wing Folding Procedure	17
13.	Fuselage Contents Arrangements	20
14.	Pre-Flight Check List	22
15.	Starting Check List	24
16.	Warm-Up Check List	26
17.	Engine Operation Check	27
18.	Magneto Operation Check	27
19.	Manifold Pressure Regulator Check	28
20.	Propeller Operation Check	29
21.	Supercharger Check	29
22.	Take-Off Check List	30
23.	Changing Power	34
24.	Supercharger Operation	35
25.	Diving Check List	36
26.	Approach and Landing Check List	38
27.	Stopping the Engine	39
28.	Mooring Diagram	40
29.	Power Plant Chart	42
30.	Air Speed Correction Table	43
31.	Cockpit Emergency Exit	44
32.	Oxygen System	46
33.	Man-Hour Oxygen Consumption Table	48
34.	GF-12/RU-17 and ZB-3 Radio Equipment	50
35.	AN/ARC-14 and AN/ARR-2 Radio Equipment	51
36.	AN/ARC-1 and AN/ARR-2a Radio Equipment	52
37.	Personnel Protection Against Gunfire	58
38.	Take-Off, Climb and Landing Chart	59
39.	Flight Operation Instruction Chart (Sheets 1 & 2)	60
40.	Angle of Attack vs. Indicated Airspeed	62
41.	Engine Calibration Curve	63

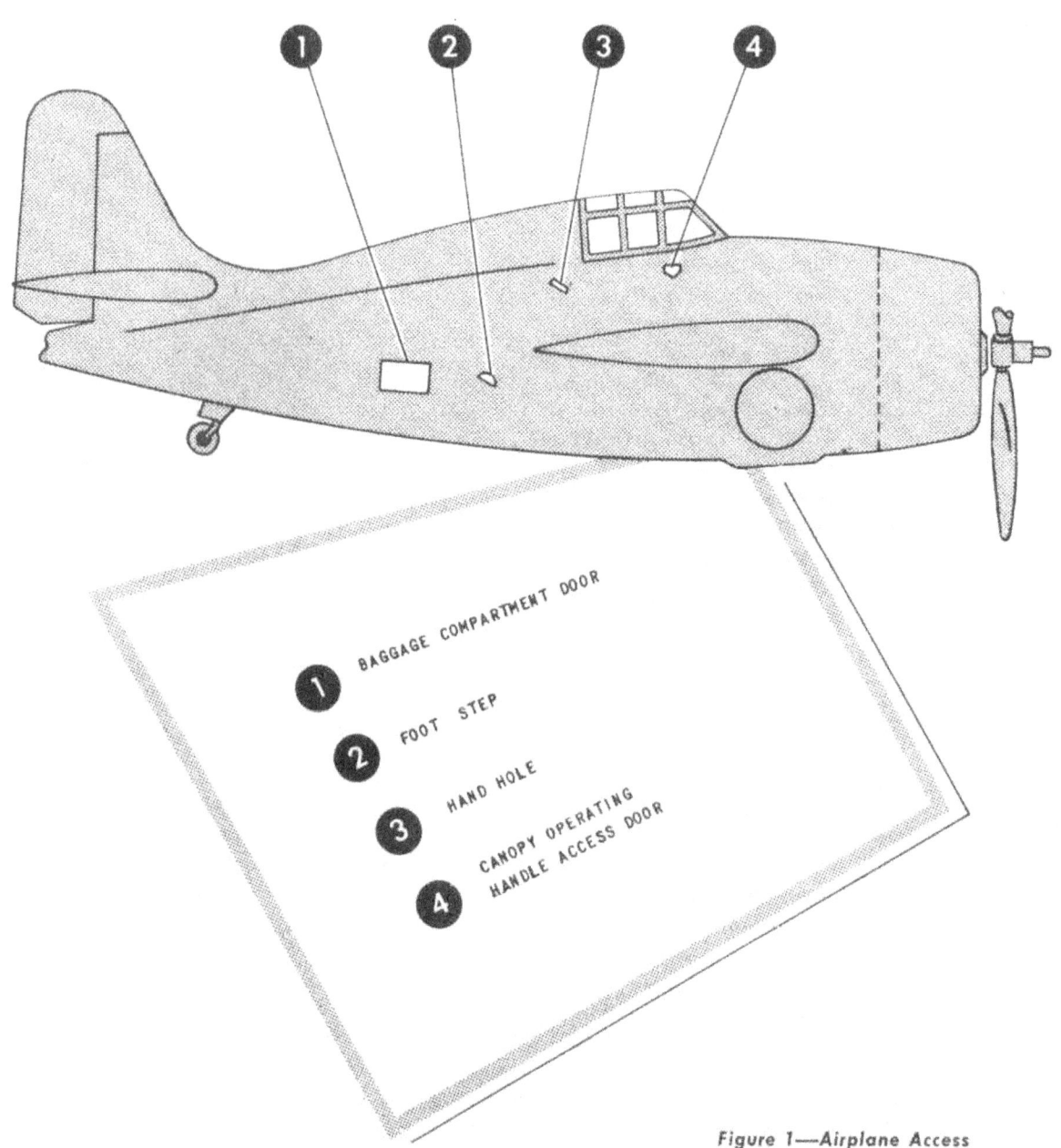

Figure 1—Airplane Access

Section 1
DESCRIPTION

1. GENERAL DESCRIPTION.

This airplane is a single engine, single place, folding mid-wing monoplane carrier fighter. The Wright R-1820-56 or -56W engine powering the plane is a nine cylinder radial with an integral two-speed, single stage supercharger. Designed to operate on Grade 100/130, AN-F-28 fuel, it has a Take-off Rating of 1300 BHP at 2600 RPM at sea level.

Starting with airplane Serial No. 57044, a Wright Anti-Detonant Injection system is installed. Preceding airplanes may have this installation. Airplanes equipped with ADI for War Emergency Power can be recognized by the Micro-switches attached to the supercharger and engine control quadrants and a take-off joggle in the throttle rail of the engine control quadrant.

The wings are folded and spread manually and are locked in the spread position by manually operated locking pins. The landing gear is mechanically retractable by the action of a handcrank operated by the pilot.

The pilot's cockpit, located above and between the wings, contains all flight, engine and auxiliary controls. See the illustrations for control locations. A baggage compartment aft of the cockpit is accessible through a hinged door on the right hand side of the airplane. This compartment houses the remote indicating compass, transmitter, radios and battery, and provides stowage area for baggage.

The airplane is equipped with four .50 caliber machine guns mounted in the outer wing panels. Armor plate, a bullet proof windshield and the engine installation combine to protect the pilot through a fifteen degree cone of fire from the front. Armor plate and structure protect the pilot through a thirty degree cone of fire from the rear.

2. SURFACE CONTROLS.

The ailerons and elevators are controlled by a standard type stick, while the rudder is operated by standard underhung pedals. These pedals are adjustable by individual levers to four positions. To adjust the pedal, place the toes on the adjustment lever and push the pedals all the way forward. With toes under the pedals, bring them aft one notch at a time until the desired position is attained. By aid of the position indicator, check that each pedal has ratcheted past the same number of notches.

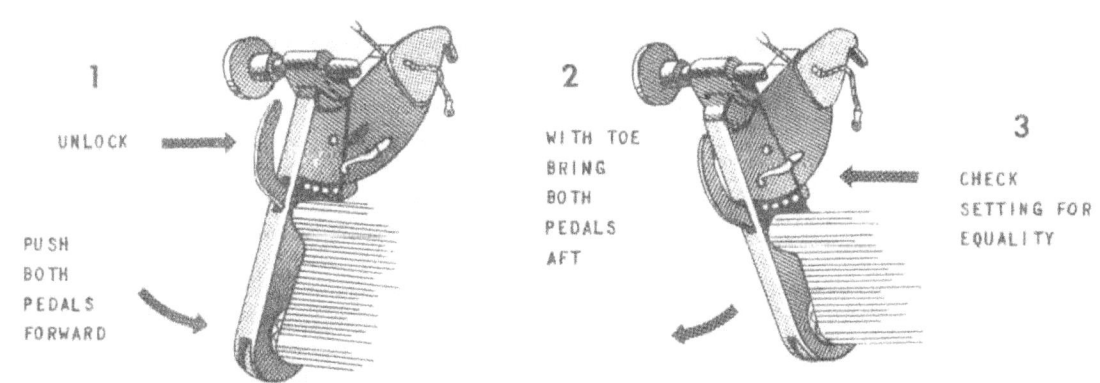

Figure 2—Pedal Adjustment Procedure

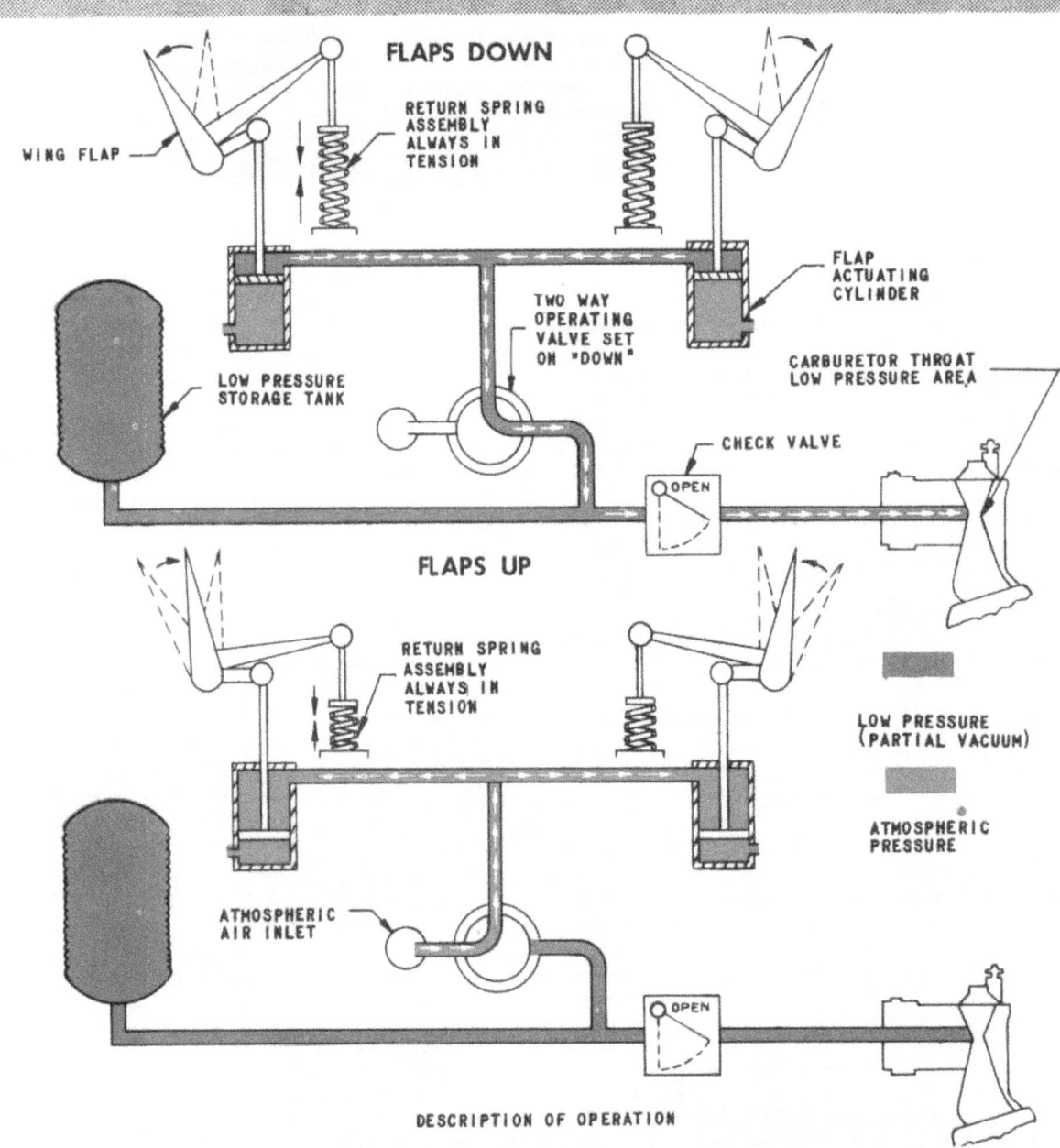

Figure 3—Wing Flap Operation

3. TAB CONTROLS.

NOTE

The tab controls are rotated in the direction of the desired resultant motion of the airplane.

a. AILERON TAB.—A cockpit controlled trim tab is provided on the left aileron only. The control wheel, which is set into the left hand shelf, is rotated counter-clockwise to lower the left wing and clockwise to lower the right wing. The tab travel is 20° up and 20° down.

A fixed tab on the right aileron is adjusted by crimping to compensate for wing inequality. A single setting on leaving the factory or following wing repair is usually sufficient. Be careful not to crimp the tab too severely as a slight change in the tab angle will compensate for considerable wing heaviness.

b. ELEVATOR TABS.—The elevator tabs are controlled by a handcrank on the side of the left hand shelf. Rotation *aft* or *counter-clockwise* raises the nose. Rotation *forward* or *clockwise* lowers the nose.

Tab travel is through a range from 6° up to 11° down. These tabs have been found effective through all ranges of loadings. Trim about the lateral axis can be checked by means of the gyro horizon.

c. RUDDER TAB.—The rudder trim tab is controlled by a wheel mounted on the left hand cockpit shelf. Rotation *clockwise* turns the nose right. Rotation *counter-clockwise* turns the nose left.

Angular travel of the tab is from 22° left to 16° tight. On take-off, a basic setting at 2½ marks in the white segment of the dial is used.

4. WING FLAP SYSTEM.

Split type wing flaps extend from the ailerons inboard to the fuselage but are divided into inboard and outboard flaps by the wing fold. Due to an overlap at the wing fold, the two sections operate as a unit capable of being drooped to a maximum of 43° by the action of a vacuum system.

The operating partial vacuum is obtained from the carburetor intake manifold and may be applied directly to the operating cylinder or stored in the vacuum tank located in the baggage compartment. This tank has sufficient capacity to operate the flaps at least twice with

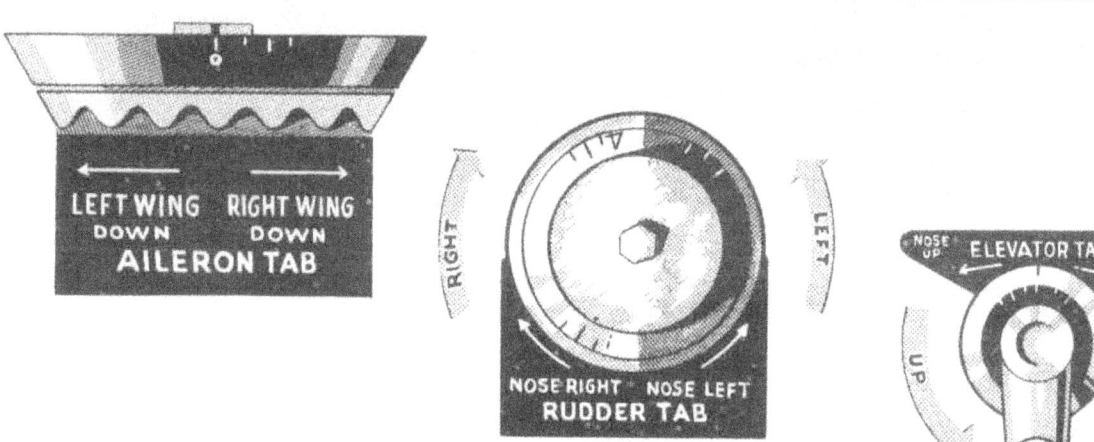

Figure 4—Tab Controls

the engine cut. Even though the switch is cut, the engine, unless it is completely stopped, will produce vacuum with the throttle closed.

The operating force on the flaps is sufficient to hold the flaps down when the engine is idled. In flight, as more power is applied and speed increases, the flaps will come up until, at about 130 knots (150 MPH), the angle of droop will be approximately 10°. If the power is then removed, the flaps will return to the *Down* position. This feature is very helpful when it is necessary to *go around again* after coming in for a landing.

In a take-off the flap valve can be left *Down* until ample speed and height are obtained for forcing flaps up. If the valve is then turned to *Up* position, any sinking effect is eliminated.

The detail operation of the system is described in the accompanying schematic diagram (Figure 4). With this vacuum system the operating efficiency of the flaps will be reduced with decreased atmospheric pressure at altitudes.

The flap operating valve control is located on the left hand shelf of the cockpit. Rotation *clockwise* for a quarter turn of the handle lowers the flaps; *counterclockwise* raises them.

5. POWER PLANT CONTROLS.

a. THROTTLE AND MIXTURE CONTROLS.—The throttle and mixture controls are united in an engine control quadrant mounted on the left hand cockpit shelf. A friction brake affecting the ease of movement of the control levers is adjusted by a knob on the face of the quadrant. The throttle is moved forward to open, aft to close. An adjustable joggle in the throttle rail marks the take-off position of the throttle control lever for the R-1820-56W engine. Movement past the take-off joggle places the throttle control in full boost position for War Emergency Power. The mixture control is moved full forward for *Auto Rich* position. *Auto Lean* position is 45° aft. *Idle Cut-Off* position, marked in red on the quadrant, is located full aft.

Fuel will be discharged from the carburetor with the mixture control in any position except *Idle Cut-Off* whenever the fuel pressure is greater than five PSI whether the engine is running or stopped. Therefore, to prevent flooding through the inadvertent use of the electric emergency fuel pump, the mixture control should always be left in the *Idle Cut-Off* position when the engine is not running. If for any reason the engine should cut out during ground operation, the mixture control should be moved immediately into the *Idle Cut-Off* position in order to prevent flooding.

For landing, all ground operations and take-off the mixture control should be set in *Auto Rich*.

For all other flight operations it is permissible to use *Auto Lean*. Satisfactory continuous operation in *Auto Lean* above Maximum cruising power is absolutely contingent upon not exceeding cylinder head temperature limits.

The positions of the mixture control for "*Auto-Rich*" and "*Idle Cut-off*" are at the fore and aft extremities, respectively, of the mixture control quadrant. The "*Auto-Lean*" position is approximately in the center of the quadrant, and must be found by seating the control in the notched position.

NOTE

Manual leaning beyond *Auto Lean* should not be attempted when operating at more than Maximum Cruising Power. Cylinder head temperature limits must be observed.

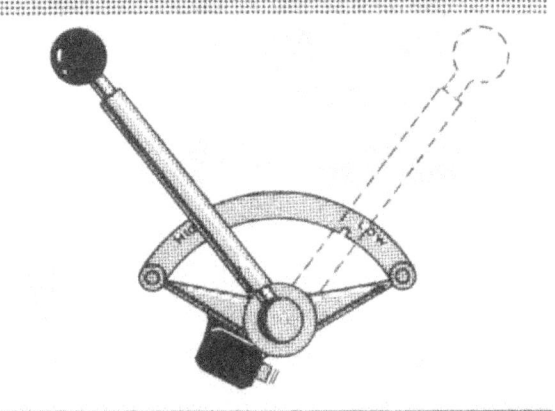

b. SUPERCHARGER CONTROL.—The two-speed

supercharger shift control is an arm mounted on a quadrant notched in two positions. To shift speed depress the knob on the top of the arm and move full forward for low blower; full aft for high blower. The control lever must be securely locked at the extremity of its travel in either *High* or *Low* position to insure complete and positive clutch engagement. Do not attempt to operate the engine with the supercharger control in any intermediate position.

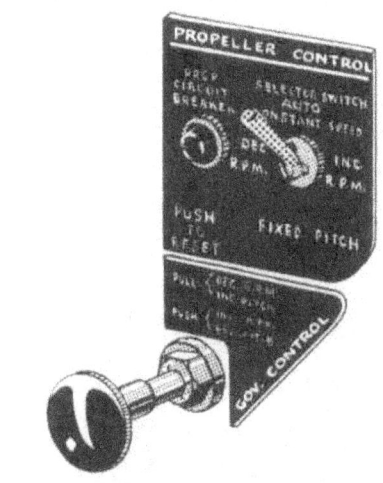

c. PROPELLER CONTROL.—The propeller is a three-blade Curtiss Electric Constant Speed type with a ten foot diameter. Basic pitch settings are at 18.5° low and 53.5° high.

Control is effected by an electric selector switch and a governor control push-pull knob.

With the selector switch in *Automatic* position, RPM is governed entirely by the operation of the push-pull knob on the left hand instrument panel. RPM is increased by pushing the knob in and decreased by pulling it out. Once an RPM is selected in this manner it will remain constant within the operating limits of the governor.

Always move the push-pull governor control knob slowly as a slight movement will cause a large change in engine RPM. For slight change in engine RPM, vernier control is recommended. This is obtained by rotating the control handle *clockwise* to increase engine RPM; *counter-clockwise* to decrease RPM.

When the selector switch is in *Fixed Pitch* position in the center of the three-way selector switch, the propeller will not be affected by movement of the control knob. For any desired manifold pressure, RPM can then be adjusted by holding the switch in either *Increase RPM* or *Decrease RPM* position until the desired RPM is obtained. Immediately on release, the switch will automatically return to *Fixed Pitch* position. Hold this RPM switch on only momentarily until the desired RPM is indicated on the tachometer.

If the circuit breaker is opened by an overload, the propeller operates at fixed pitch at the pitch angle in effect at the moment the breaker is opened. Fixed pitch control cannot be used with this circuit breaker open; the propeller blade angle cannot be changed until the circuit breaker is reset.

AUTOMATIC CONTROL

To Increase RPM

    Circuit Breaker..On
    Selector Switch..Automatic
    Propeller Governor Knob..............................Push In

To Decrease RPM

    Circuit Breaker..On
    Selector Switch..Automatic
    Propeller Governor Knob..............................Pull Out

FIXED PITCH CONTROL

To Increase RPM

    Circuit Breaker..On
    Selector Switch..Fixed Pitch
    Selector Switch......................................Increase RPM

To Decrease RPM

    Circuit Breaker..On
    Selector Switch..Fixed Pitch
    Selector Switch.....................................Decrease RPM

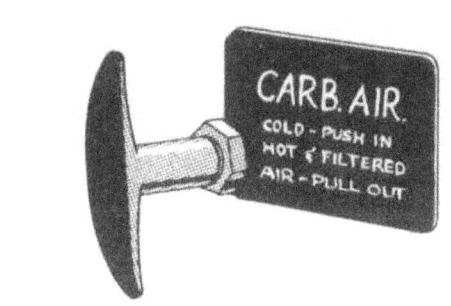

d. CARBURETOR AIR CONTROL.—The carburetor air control handle is located on the left hand instrument panel to the right of the propeller control. The full-in position allows direct cold air from the atmosphere to be taken in through the air scoop and enter the carburetor at the same time preventing warm air from entering the carburetor. The full-out position prevents the direct cold air from entering the carburetor but allows the warm air to be taken in from the accessory section. This control operates a door whose action may be compared to a two-way valve.

Never use an intermediate position for this control. The control should be left in *Direct (Cold)* position at all times unless icing conditions are suspected or rain is encountered. Under these conditions the control should be pulled out to the *Alternate Hot* position.

e. COWL FLAP CONTROL AND CYLINDER HEAD TEMPERATURES.—The cowl flaps are operated by a handcrank located on the right hand instrument panel. Rotation *clockwise* closes the flaps; rotation *counter-clockwise* opens them.

The full open setting of the cowl flaps is provided primarily for ground cooling. Intermediate settings should be used as needed so that the following cylinder head temperatures will not be exceeded:

War Emergency Power..........248°C (478°F) (5 min.)
Take-Off ....248°C (478°F) (5 min.)
Military Power ....232°C (450°F) (30 min.)
Normal Rated Power:
  ....232°C (450°F) (1 hour)
  ....218°C (424°F) (Cont.)
Maximum Cruising Power
  and Below..........................205°C (401°F) (Cont.)

NOTE

As the cowl flaps create a considerable drag when open as shown in the following table, they should be opened gradually in level flight as the temperature approaches the limit, rather than all the way when the limit is reached.

In a climb increase the airspeed by as much as 10 knots in preference to opening them more than half way.

	COWL FLAP DRAG IN KNOTS	
IAS	½ OPEN	FULL OPEN
120	8	15
140	7	14
160	7	13
180	7	13
200	6	12
220	5	11

Cylinder head temperatures can be reduced by:
1. Enriching the mixture.
2. Opening cowl flaps.
3. Reducing power.
4. Increasing climbing air speed.

f. IGNITION SWITCH.—The four position ignition switch is located on the left hand instrument panel. The *Left* and *Right* positions are used in checking the two magnetos during the engine warm-up period. The procedure is outlined in Section II, Paragraph 7c.

g. PRIMING SYSTEM AND CONTROL.—An electrically controlled priming system draws fuel from the carburetor and injects it into the diffuser section of the engine in two places. The primer switch is located on the pilot's distribution panel adjacent to the starter switch so that both may be operated with one hand. The primer switch is to be held down only momentarily, i.e. for not more than three to five seconds. Upon release it automatically returns to the *Off* position.

h. STARTER AND CONTROL.—A Breeze Type I cartridge starter is fired electrically by the starter switch. This switch is located on the pilot's distribution panel adjacent to the primer switch. To operate this switch, it is necessary to raise the guard and hold the switch in

Figure 5—Instrument Panel

1. CYLINDER HEAD TEMPERATURE GAUGE
2. IGNITION SWITCH
3. CLOCK
4. WINDSHIELD DEFROSTER CONTROL
5. PROPELLER GOVERNOR CONTROL
6. PROPELLER SELECTOR SWITCH AND CIRCUIT BREAKER
7. GUN SIGHT SWITCH AND RHEOSTAT
8. CARBURETOR AIR CONTROL
9. LOW LEVEL FUEL WARNING LIGHT
10. FUEL QUANTITY GAUGE
11. EMERGENCY FUEL PUMP SWITCH
12. ALTIMETER
13. DIRECTIONAL GYRO
14. AIRSPEED INDICATOR
15. TURN AND BANK INDICATOR
16. CLIMB INDICATOR
17. GYRO HORIZON
18. MANIFOLD PRESSURE GAUGE
19. TACHOMETER
20. OXYGEN FLOW METER
21. OIL DILUTION SWITCH
22. ENGINE GAUGE UNIT
23. COWL FLAP CONTROL HANDLE
24. PEDAL ADJUSTMENT LEVERS
25. RUDDER PEDALS
26. CHART BOARD
27. CONTROL STICK
28. COMPASS
29. CABIN AIR INTAKE CONTROL

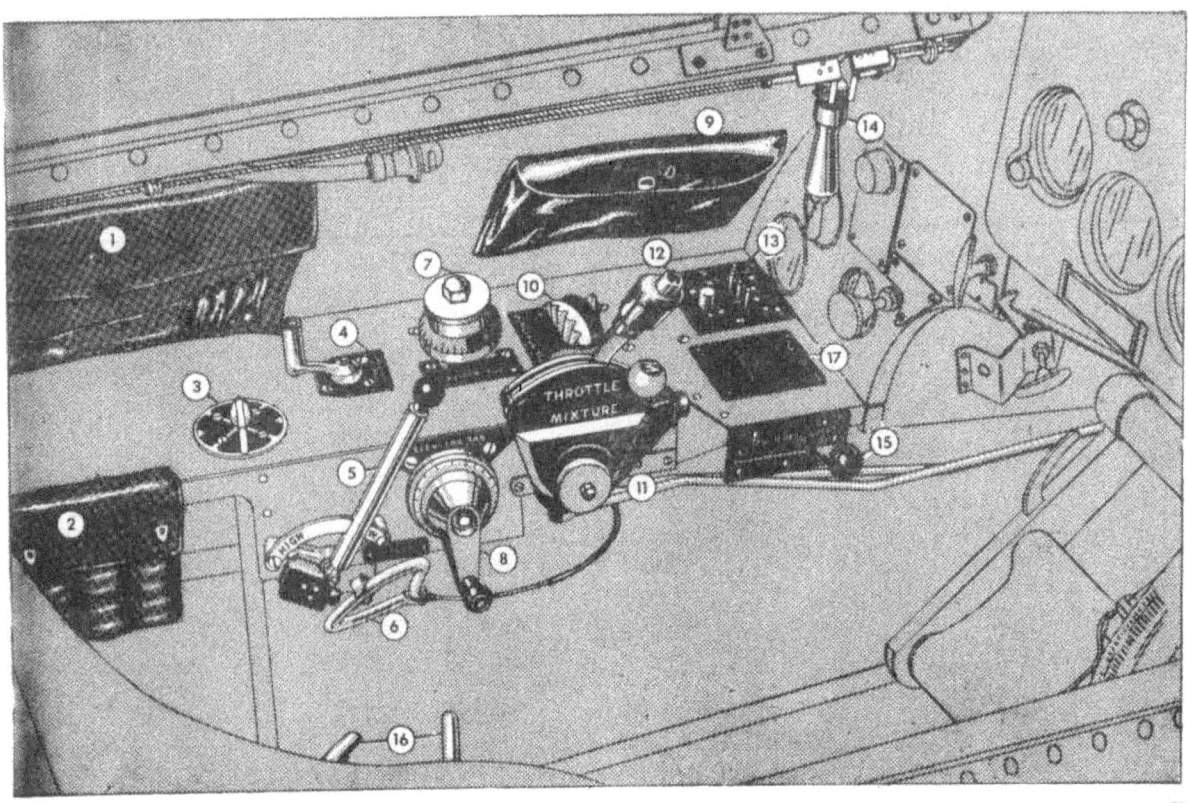

1. MAP CASE
2. PYROTECHNIC CARTRIDGE CASE
3. FUEL TANK SELECTOR VALVE
4. LANDING FLAP CONTROL
5. SUPERCHARGER CONTROL QUADRANT
6. DROPPABLE FUEL TANK RELEASE HANDLE
7. RUDDER TAB CONTROL
8. ELEVATOR TAB CONTROL
9. WIRING DIAGRAM POCKET
10. AILERON TAB CONTROL
11. THROTTLE AND MIXTURE CONTROL QUADRANT
12. THROAT MICROPHONE SWITCH
13. RECOGNITION LIGHT SWITCHES
14. ARRESTING HOOK CONTROL HANDLE
15. TAIL WHEEL LOCK CONTROL
16. GUN CHARGING HANDLES
17. CHECK OFF LIST

Figure 6—Left Hand Side of Cockpit

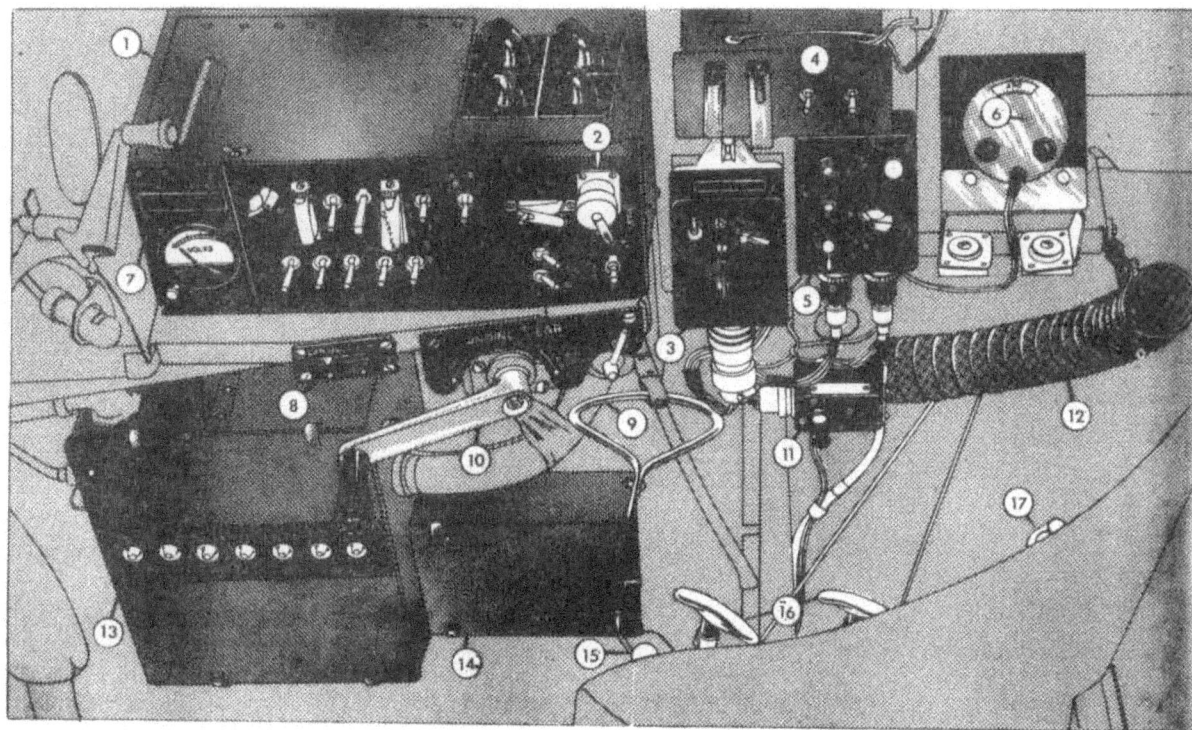

1. PILOT'S DISTRIBUTION PANEL
2. POWER RECEPTACLE (FOR ELECTRICALLY HEATED SUITS)
3. COMMUNICATION EQUIPMENT CONTROL UNIT
4. IFF CONTROL BOX
5. NAVIGATION EQUIPMENT CONTROL UNIT
6. RANGE RECEIVER
7. VOLT-AMMETER
8. LANDING GEAR POSITION INDICATOR
9. DROPPABLE FUEL TANK RELEASE HANDLE
10. LANDING GEAR HANDCRANK
11. JACK BOX
12. COCKPIT VENTILATOR
13. MAIN JUNCTION BOX AND CIRCUIT BREAKER RESET BUTTONS
14. GENERATOR CUT-OUT
15. PILOT'S SEAT ADJUSTMENT HANDLE
16. RIGHT HAND GUN CHARGING HANDLES
17. OXYGEN BOTTLE SHUT-OFF VALVE

Figure 7— Right Hand Side of Cockpit

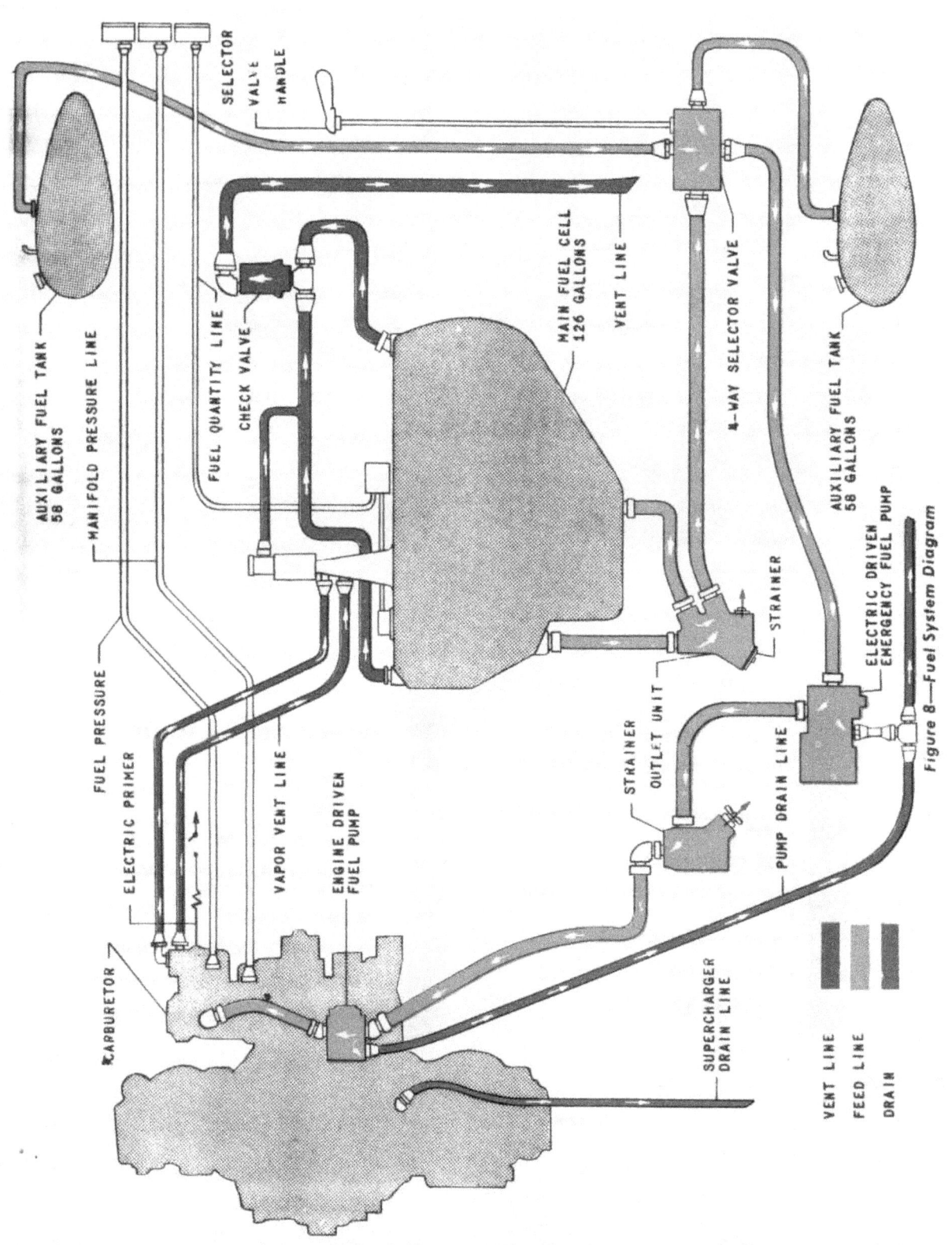

Figure 8 — Fuel System Diagram

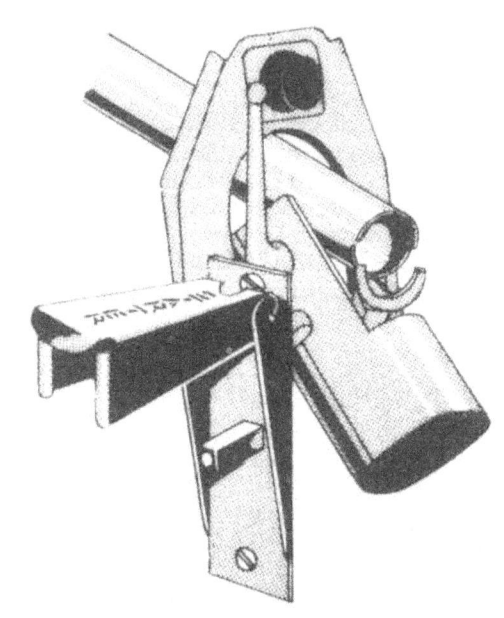

TANK CAPACITIES

Main Tank......117 U.S. (97 Imp.) Gals. (with liner)
               130 U.S. (108 Imp.) Gals. (without liner)
Airplane No. 57044 and subsequent
  Main Cell......................126 U.S. (105 Imp.) Gals.
Droppable, Right......................58 U. S. (48 Imp.) Gals.
Droppable, Left......................58 U. S. (48 Imp.) Gals.

Fuel should be drawn from the main tank for a short time before switching to the droppable tanks. Fuel may be drawn from either droppable tank but the pilot should compensate for loss of weight on the one wing as the fuel is used by means of the trim tabs. Trim tab adjustment will compensate for a full tank on one wing and an empty tank on the other.

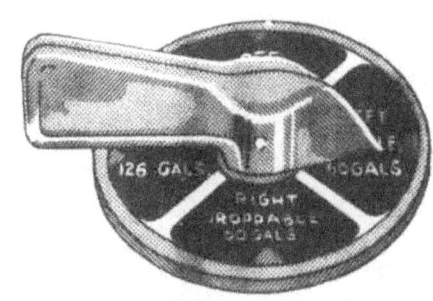

the "ON" position; it automatically returns to the "OFF" position upon release. The battery switch must be "ON" to operate the starter.

The starter breech is located on the right hand side of the engine mount structure and is accessible from the outside through the right hand landing gear well. Type C cartridges are to be used under all circumstances. A box containing extra cartridges is mounted in the engine accessory section on the engine mount support tubing.

NOTE

The starter switch need not be held *ON* after the cartridge is fired as there is no booster coil in this airplane.

6. FUEL SYSTEM.

a. DESCRIPTION.—The fuel system is basically a single tank pressure feed system with provisions for two auxiliary droppable tanks, one under each wing. The main tank, located in the fuselage below the cockpit, is equipped with a self-sealing liner. On airplane No. 57044 and subsequent the main tank although located in the same position consists only of a rigid self-sealing fuel cell without an aluminum shell.

Fuel grade 100/130, Specification AN-F-28, is specified.

b. TANK SELECTOR VALVE.—The tank selector valve, located on the left hand cockpit shelf, has four positions: *Main, Left Droppable, Right Droppable,* and *Off*. The fuel tank selector should always be set on *Main* for take-off and landing. Always turn on the emergency fuel pump when changing fuel tanks.

c. ELECTRIC EMERGENCY FUEL PUMP.—An electric emergency fuel pump is installed in the fuel system in place of the more common manually operated wobble pump. This emergency pump is controlled by an electric switch set in the left hand instrument panel. It should be used when starting, when changing fuel tanks, and when necessary to maintain fuel pressure in case of failure of the engine driven pump or of lowered fuel pressure at high altitudes.

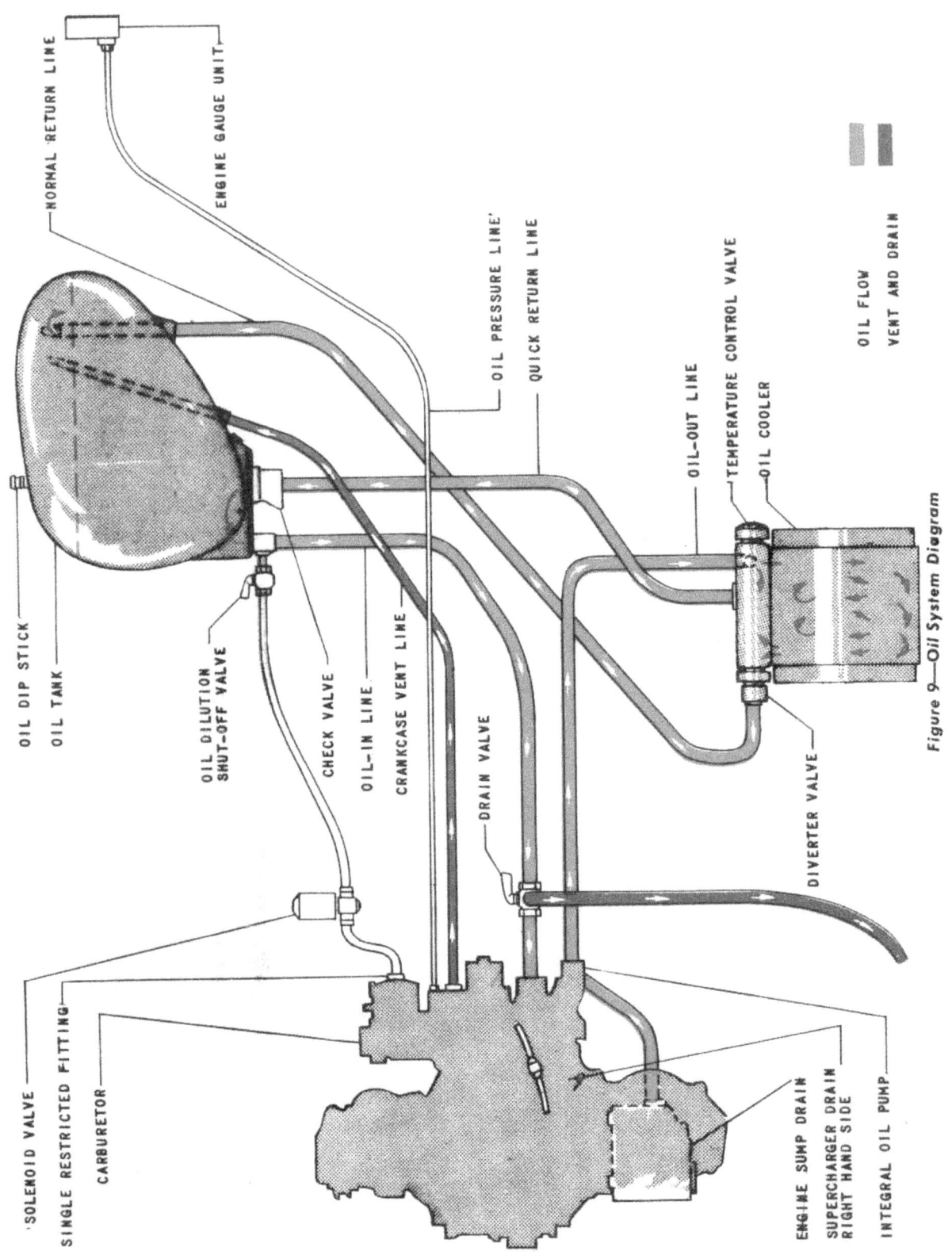

Figure 9 — *Oil System Diagram*

d. FUEL QUANTITY GUAGE.—An electric fuel quantity gauge with the indicator mounted in the right hand panel shows the fuel level in the main tank only. No gauge is provided for the droppable tanks, therefore fuel consumption from these tanks must be determined from the lapsed time during which fuel is withdrawn.

e. LOW FUEL LEVEL WARNING LIGHT.—On airplane No. 57044 and subsequent, a low fuel level red warning light is installed on the left hand instrument panel next to the fuel quantity gage which is also installed on the left hand panel beginning with this installation. This light goes on when only 30 gallons of fuel (a minimum of one-half hour of flying time at Cruising Power) are left in the main tank.

f. DROPPABLE FUEL TANK RELEASE.—Droppable fuel tank release handles are red painted rings, one located on each side of the cockpit on the sides of the shelves. A sharp pull releases the tanks. The handles should then be clipped back to shelves in their former position to prevent them from fouling other controls.

g. VAPOR RETURN.—The vapor return line from the carburetor to the main tank may return as much as eight gallons of fuel per hour. Consequently, when operating with all tanks full, use about fifteen gallons of fuel from the main tank before turning the selector to one of the droppable tanks. This is necessary to make room for the returned fuel which otherwise would overflow out through the vent line.

7. OIL SYSTEM.

a. DESCRIPTION.—The oil supply is carried in a single tank attached to the upper engine mount. It is distributed by an engine driven oil pump and returned by scavenger pumps located in the engine nose sump and rear case.

TANK CAPACITY
Normal .... 9 U.S. (7.5 Imp.) Gals.
Overload ....11 U.S. (9.0 Imp.) Gals.

Oil grade 1120, Specification AN-VV-O-446, should be used. The recommended grade of oil varies with temperature. The latest service instructions and technical orders should be followed.

Oil returning from the engine passes through a thermostatic regulator valve mounted on the oil cooler. This valve causes the oil to by-pass the cooler until the oil-in temperature reaches 21°C (70°F) at which time the valve starts to open and then maintains the desired oil-in temperature range of 75°C to 90°C (167°F to 194F°). Cold oil by-passing the cooler is discharged into the tank adjacent to the suction outlet leading to the oil pump. Much of the same oil is thereby kept in circulation, hastening the rise of the oil-in temperature.

b. OIL DILUTION SYSTEM.—The system consists of a solenoid valve electrically operated by a momentary switch on the right hand instrument panel, a single restricted fitting, and a safety shut-off cock located in the dilution line between the carburetor and oil tank suction outlet leading to the oil pump.

The Oil Dilution switch is also connected to a second solenoid which simultaneously operates a diverter valve in the temperature regulator valve. This enables the diluted oil to by-pass the cooler and return to the bottom of the oil tank near the suction outlet.

Refer to Section II, Paragraph 20*b* for operational instructions for the oil dilution system.

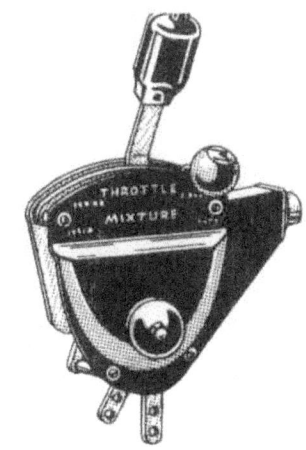

8. ANTI-DETONANT INJECTION SYSTEM.

Figure 10 schematically outlines the general arrangement of the ADI system as installed in this airplane with the R1820-56W engine. The fluid tank located in the accessory compartment, contains a ten minute supply of fluid, pressurized through a boost pressure supply line. A check valve incorporated in the line prevents loss of tank pressure when manifold pressure is reduced following Take-off.

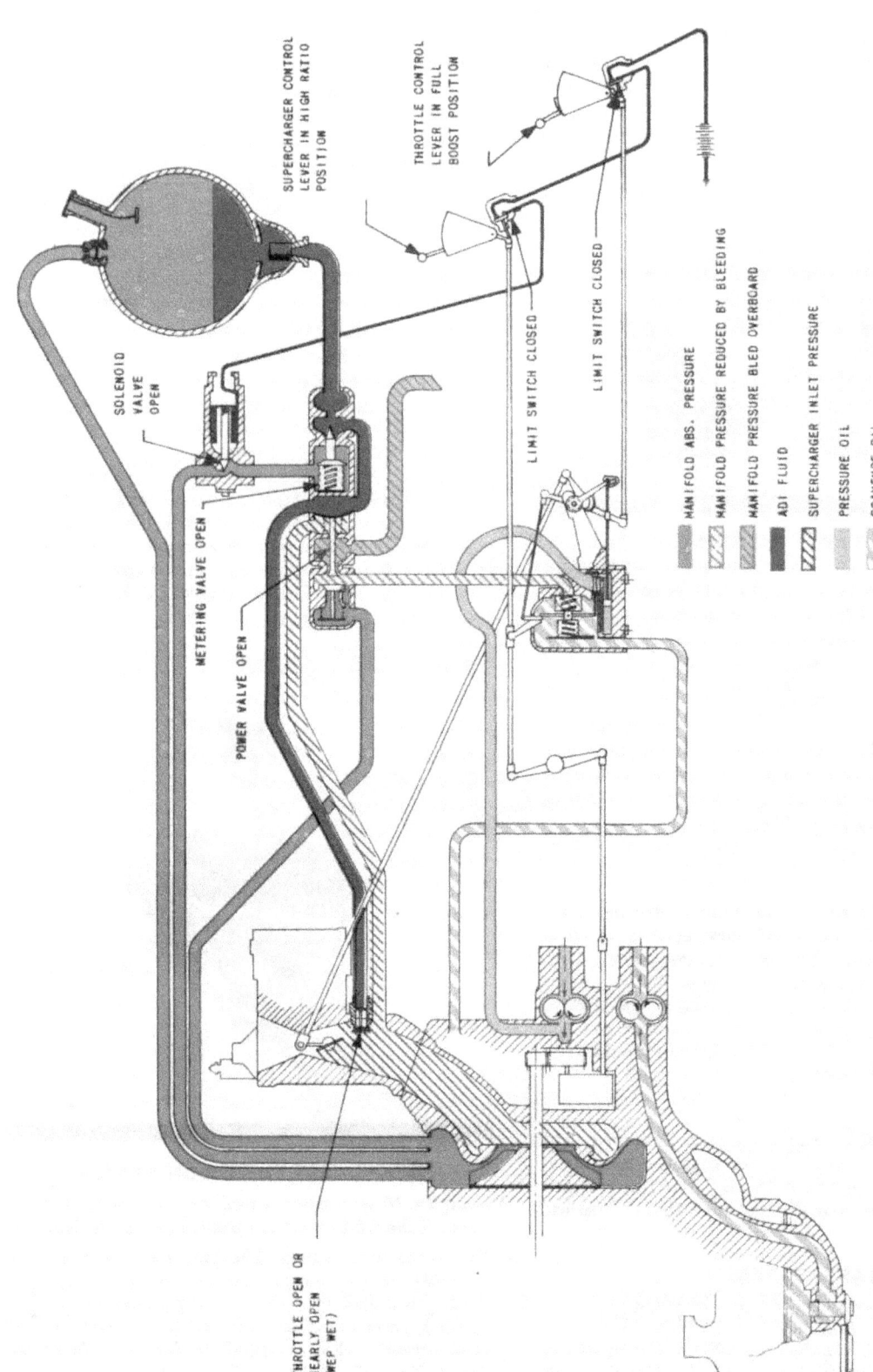

Figure 10—ADI System Schematic Diagram

The MP Regulator and ADI Control Unit are mounted together on an assembly bracket. The solenoid valve, which controls the start of ADI operation, is actuated by two switches placed in series to prevent undesired fluid flow. One switch is mounted on the supercharger control quadrant so that movement of the lever into High Blower position closes this switch. The second switch is mounted on the cockpit shelf so that movement of throttle control lever past the Take-off stop will close the switch completing the circuit to inaugurate ADI operation.

9. LANDING GEAR CONTROLS.

a. RETRACTING MECHANISM.—The landing gear is retracted or extended manually by means of a handcrank located on the right side of the cockpit. Approximately twenty-eight turns of the crank are required to raise or lower the landing gear. The crank is rotated *clockwise* to raise the gear and *counter-clockwise* to lower it.

WARNING

While extending the wheels, a point is reached at which it becomes more difficult to rotate the crank handle and there may be a tendency for the pilot to stop and engage the ratchet lock. However, the pilot should continue to rotate the crank handle until it hits a stop indicating that the gear is fully down.

The handcrank is automatically latched by a ratchet acting on the crank while the wheels are being raised or lowered. The ratchet is released by operating a small lever just aft of the handcrank. After releasing the ratchet lever, the crank remains locked until pressure is exerted on the crank opposite to the desired direction of rotation.

b. HANDCRANK BRAKE.—The landing gear handcrank brake is installed on the operating shaft just forward of the handcrank gear box. This unit ratchets when the landing gear is being raised. When the gear is being lowered, a pawl engages the drum and the braking action retards the speed with which the wheels are lowered. The single adjusting nut which regulates the tension on the friction brake must be so adjusted that the lowering speed of the wheels will not tear the handcrank from the pilot's hand and possibly strip the gears. Proper adjustment will prevent this but as an additional precaution the pilot *must retain a firm grip* on the crank handle.

c. POSITION OF WHEELS.—The mechanical position indicator just forward of the handcrank on the right hand shelf shows the approximate position of the wheels. However, the only definite check lies in full rotation of the handle in the correct direction as far as it will go.

d. EXTENDED POSITION LOCK.—With the wheels cranked to *Full-Down* position, sufficient locking force is exerted by the large operating chains, supplemented by a spring counterbalance unit, to prevent all possibility of wheels retracting during landing and take-off.

No adjustment is necessary on the counterbalance unit. It is so designed that it will always exert the proper force.

e. BRAKE CONTROL.—The duo-servo hydraulic brakes are operated by toe pressure on the upper part of the rudder pedals.

f. ARRESTING HOOK CONTROL.—The arresting hook located in the after fuselage is operated through

a system of cables by a control mounted in a slide under the left hand cockpit rail.

To lower the hook rotate the handle up, pull it aft, and rotate the handle down. To raise the hook, reverse the procedure. About a twenty pound push is required to retract the hook.

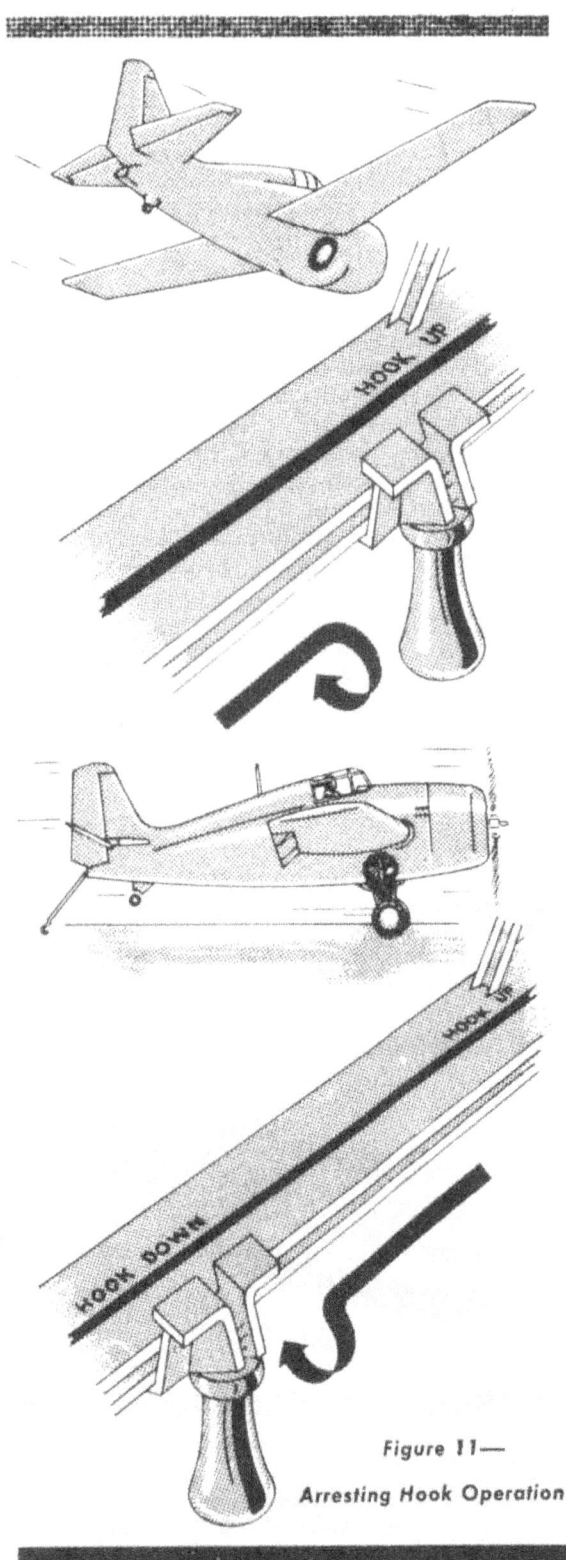

Figure 11—
Arresting Hook Operation

WARNING

The pilot shall insure that the control handle is locked in the hook-down position prior to landing aboard a carrier.

The approach light automatically goes on when the arresting hook is lowered. A manual switch for the approach light is provided in the after fuselage for use in practicing carrier landings.

g. TAIL WHEEL CASTER LOCK.—The tail wheel drag link is equipped with a lock pin which locks the caster in the trailing position. This lock pin is controlled by a cable from the *Tail Wheel Lock* lever on the port cockpit shelf. With the lever in the forward position, the tail wheel is locked; in the aft position the tail wheel is free to swivel, i.e. unlocked.

The primary purpose of this lock is to reduce the possibility of ground looping on landing. Lock the tail wheel immediately after taxiing into position for take-off. The tail wheel will then remain locked during flight and during landing. Unlock the wheel after the landing run has been completed in order to facilitate taxiing.

For carrier operation, leave the tail wheel unlocked.

The tail wheel is a 360° swivel type equipped with a spring-loaded, self-centering device. The tire is a high-pressure type. Pressure should be kept at 110 pounds for normal operation and 175 pounds for carrier operation.

10. WING FOLDING.

a. CONTROLS.—The wings are folded and spread manually from the ground and are held in spread position by locking pins operated by handcranks. These handcranks are stowed in the leading edges of the wing at the folding axes and are reached through doors secured by latches.

b. SAFETY INDICATOR.—As the locking pins are withdrawn, red metal flags are raised above the upper surface of the stub panel in each wing. *The pilot should never take-off when any portion of either red flag shows above the wing surface without investigating the wing lock.*

c. TO FOLD WINGS.—Open the cover doors at the wing fold and set the handcranks. Turn the handcranks *counter-clockwise* to withdraw the locking pins. Move the wings to folded position and set the jury struts or cables into the fittings in the wing tips and outboard end of the stabilizers. The two sets of jury struts, cable and bar, are stowed in the baggage compartment of the airplane.

d. TO SPREAD WINGS.—Remove the jury struts. One man turns the locking pin crank handle fully counter-clockwise to make sure the locking pin is in the unlocked or fully out position. A second man then moves the wing into a spread position by pushing on the wing tip. While the wing is being held in the full spread position, the first man advances the locking pin to a locked position by clockwise rotation of the handcrank. Continue cranking until the pin is in as far as it will go and no part of the red warning flag appears above the wing surface. Fold and stow the handcrank and snap the cover door closed.

CAUTION

When unlocking to fold the wings or releasing cables to spread wings, the wing will swing dangerously fast to a drooped position unless restraint is placed on the wing tip. If the wing is allowed to swing free and the arc is misjudged, damage may result to plane or personnel.

11. ARMAMENT CONTROLS.

a. GUNNERY CONTROLS.

(1) GENERAL DESCRIPTION.—Two .50 caliber machine guns and ammunition boxes are mounted in each wing outer panel. The guns are charged manually and fired electrically.

(2) GUN CHARGING.—Charging handle for each gun is located beside the pilot's seat, two each outboard of the right and left floor channels. Pull upward and return to load each gun. The shell is then under the hammer ready to fire. Guns need be charged manually only once after installing the boxes and catching the first shell behind the belt holding pawl.

By rotating the handle left or right while extended to charge position, the handle can be locked in full charge or an intermediate safety position to make it possible to operate safely with a shell in the chamber during catapulting or landing operations.

(3) GUN FIRING.—The guarded gun master switch marked *Guns* and the gun selector switches are mounted on the pilot's distribution panel on the right cockpit shelf. The trigger switch is incorporated in the control stick handle.

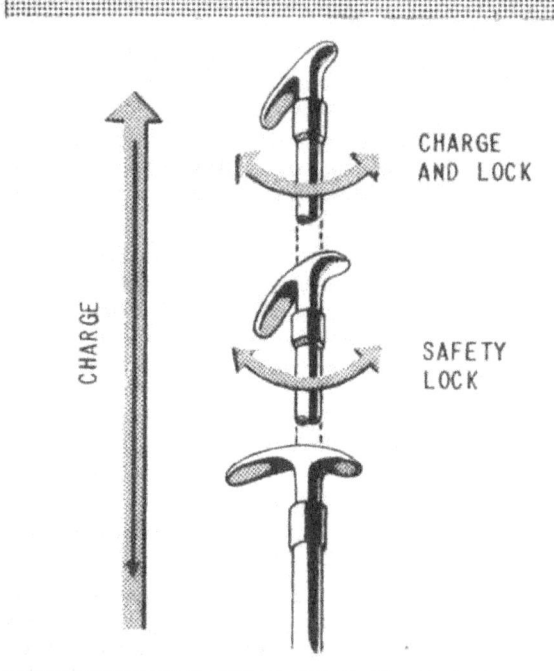

The master switch must be on to fire the guns. By use of the selector switches, the guns can be fired as a battery or in outboard and inboard pairs. Closing the trigger switch completes the firing circuit. Due to longer chutes and deeper boxes, the inboard guns carry slightly more ammunition than the outboard guns.

Individual fuses for each gun circuit are located in the top of the distribution panel. Spare fuses for replacement are contained in sockets directly under the active fuses.

(4) GUN SIGHTS.—The Mark VIII gun sight is controlled by a switch and rheostat mounted on the left

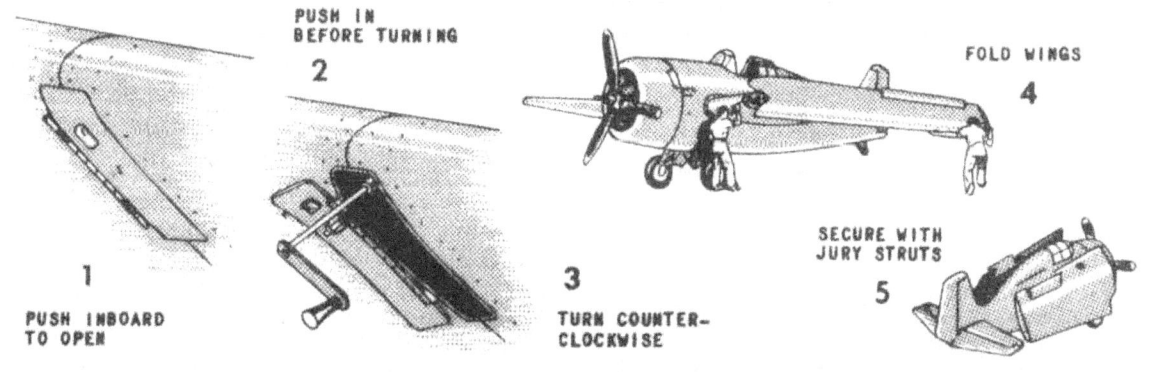

Figure 12—Wing Folding Procedure

instrument panel. The sight operates independently of the gun master switch.

To use the sight set the switch *On* and turn on the rheostat. If the bulb does not illuminate, turn the switch to *On Alternate* to use the spare filament.

The gun sight circuit contains a circuit breaker with the reset button mounted in the main junction box cover just below the distribution panel. In case of overload, reset the circuit breaker by pushing the reset button.

(5) GUN CAMERA.—The gun camera, type AN-N-4, is mounted in the leading edge of the port wing stub. The control switch is mounted on the pilot's distribution panel. The gun camera heating element is always *On* when the gun camera is being operated as it is controlled by the gun camera switch. The gun camera switch which works independently of the gun master switch *must* be *On* to operate the camera.

Pictures are taken by the camera only when the trigger switch is squeezed by the pilot.

Fuses for the gun camera circuit are located under the cover of the distribution panel.

(6) ELECTRIC GUN HEATERS.—Electric gun heaters of the pad type may be installed over each gun breech. A junction box is provided on the inboard side of the inboard gun compartment in each wing for this installation. The electric circuit is connected directly to the generator and the heaters are on at all times when the plug is connected to the junction box and the engine is running.

b. ROCKET INSTALLATION.

(1) The rocket installation in the FM-2 consists of three Mk 5 Series Aircraft Rocket Launchers mounted on the undersurface of each wing. The wiring necessary includes a Mk 3 or Mk 3-1 Station Distributor and a firing switch. The later is the button on the top of the control stick normally used for the bomb release circuit. The station distributor is located below the instrument panel forward of the control stick. Each launcher consists of 2 streamlined posts; the forward post contains a fuse arming control and the aft post contains both a receptacle for the rocket firing lead and a latch to restrain the rocket until the instant of firing.

WARNING

If the pilot is in the airplane at the time the rocket firing leads are connected, he should be certain that the master armament switch is OFF and that the station distributor "safety" plug is removed.

(2) When the airplane is airborne and heading away from friendly installations or approaching a target range, the switches should be turned *ON;* The indicator light on the station distributor will glow when all switches are on; the intensity of the light may be varied by turning the knob on the light (which regulates a shutter). The station distributor switches should be turned off before the airplane returns to its base.

(3) The *SAFE-ARM* switch on the station distributor must be in the *ARM* position to allow the instantaneous nose fuse to arm and in the *SAFE* position to allow the short delay fuse to function. When the base fuse only is allowed to function, the rocket will penetrate the target before exploding.

(4) When the *SINGLE-AUTO* switch on the station distributor is set on *SINGLE,* a pair of rockets will be fired each time the trigger switch is depressed; when the switch is on the *AUTO* position, pairs of rockets will be fired at automatically spaced intervals (0.3 sec. with the Mk. 3, 0.1 sec with the Mk. 3-1) while the switch is held closed.

c. TOW TARGET.—There is provision for the installation of a tow target release control on the right hand cockpit floor channel as marked by a name plate and for a release latch on the bottom of the fuselage. Refer to the Erection and Maintenance Manual for installation details. The tow target is released by an upward pull on the handle.

d. PYROTECHNICS.—There are provisions for a pyrotechnic pistol in the cockpit floor to the right of the pilot. Extra cartridges for the pistol are contained in a holder on the left hand cockpit shelf just aft of the supercharger control.

12. ELECTRICAL SYSTEM.

a. GENERAL DESCRIPTION.—The electrical system of this airplane is of the conventional single wire design. The active fuses, spare fuses and spare bulbs are stowed under the cover of the pilot's distribution panel. A standard receptacle is also provided in the rear upper corner of the distribution panel.

With three exceptions, all electrical equipment including the aforementioned receptacle, is connected to the positive bus bar in the distribution panel and therefore is hot whenever the engine is running, i.e. electricity is being generated by the generator and/or when the battery master switch is *On* or closed.

The three exceptions to the above are the gun heaters, the radio destructor switch, and the recognition lights. The gun heaters are connected to the generator side of the cut-out and therefore are only *On* when the engine is running and work independently of the battery. The radio destructor switch and the recognition light switch are connected to the battery side of the battery switch and therefore are always *Hot*.

Starting with airplane serial No. 57044 and subsequent a Generator Field switch is mounted on the distribution panel. This switch is normally *On* and is to be put *Off* only in emergency if the generator voltage regulator fails and it is desirous to cut-out the generator field to prevent damage to the battery and possibly other equipment.

The generator cut-out is located aft of the main junction box under the distribution panel.

The volt-ammeter is located on the forward face of the distribution panel.

b. ELECTRICAL CONTROLS.—The electrical controls, unless otherwise stated in a specific paragraph are all located on the distribution panel on the right hand cockpit shelf. The following controls are mounted on the panel:

SWITCHES

Section Light	Gun Camera
Formation Lights	Pitot Tube Heat
Flash Switch	Starter
Wing Running Lights	Primer
Tail Running Lights	Battery
Gun Master Switch	Gun Selector Switches (2)

Ship No. 57044 and Subsequent:

Generator Field Switch	Master Radio Switch

RHEOSTATS

Electric Panel Light	Instrument Panel Lights
Cockpit Lights	
Compass Light	Chart Board Light

c. COCKPIT LIGHTING.—The cockpit and instruments are lighted by a right and left cockpit light, a compass light, a chartboard light, seven instrument panel lights, and a panel light. Spare bulbs are stowed as described above. The lights are controlled by rheostats with an *Off* position mounted on the pilot's distribution panel.

d. SPECIAL LIGHTING.—The section and formation lights have individual *Bright-Off-Dim* switches and one common *Flash-Off-On* switch. To operate the lights the combined switch must be on *On* or *Flash,* and the individual switches set for either *Dim* or *Bright.*

An approach light manual switch is built into the approach light switch box just forward of Station 13 in the baggage compartment. This manual switch is in parallel with the automatic switch tripped by the arresting hook, and is used only for practice carrier landings

RESTRICTED
AN 01-190FB-1

THIS PAGE INTENTIONALLY LEFT BLANK.

without actually letting the hook down. This switch must be turned on before taking off from the airport.

The recognition lights toggle switches and keying switch are on the forward end of the left hand cockpit shelf.

13. AUXILIARY CONTROLS.

a. SLIDING CANOPY.

(1) OPERATION.—The sliding canopy is operated by means of a large handle mounted in a slide on the right hand side of the cockpit under the cockpit rail. The handle is rotated upward and pulled aft to open the enclosure. By rotating downwards, the handle may be latched in any one of four positions: Closed, 1¼ inches Open, 5⅜ inches Open, and Full Open. An angle clip on the lower left corner of the canopy may be used to assist in opening and in closing the canopy. A small door in the right hand side of the fuselage just below the windshield gives access to the cockpit from outside for the purpose of operating the handle when the canopy is closed.

(2) EMERGENCY RELEASE.—The trolley slides at the forward end of the canopy are fastened to the canopy proper by quick release latches. These latches consist of pins joining the slide and the canopy. The release pins should be kept lubricated with a thin coating of grease at all times to permit easy removal. See Figure 31 and Section IV, Paragraph 1, for emergency release operating instructions.

b. WINDSHIELD DEFROSTER.—A T-handle control for the windshield heat defroster is located above the left rudder pedal just forward and below the instrument panel. To introduce heat into the air space between the double windshield, pull the handle aft.

c. COCKPIT AIR INTAKE.—A toe operated valve located at the base of the compass mount forward of the

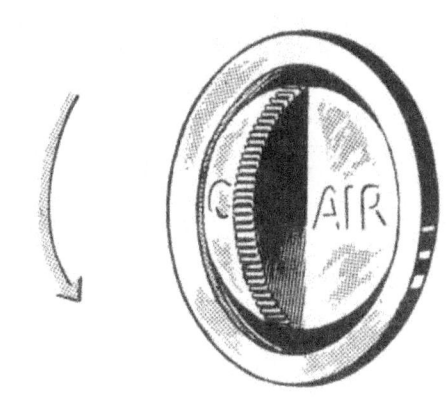

control stick introduces fresh air into the pilot's cockpit from an intake in the right hand stub wing.

d. PILOT'S SEAT ADJUSTMENT.—A control lever for the vertical adjustment of the pilot's seat is located on the right hand side of the seat. Movement aft releases the locking pin in the seat stanchion and allows the pilot to lower the seat by body weight, or raise it through the tension of the shock cords to any one of seven positions.

e. SHOULDER HARNESS.—The control lever on the left hand side of the seat locks the shoulder type harness. The Sutton shoulder harness should be connected to the spring on the rear of the pilot's seat. When the locking handle on the left hand side of the seat is in the aft position, this spring allows the pilot unrestricted movement. Moving the handle forward locks the harness spring. To move the handle, the knob should first be depressed.

In installing the harness, pass the shoulder straps *over* the bar just below the pilot's headrest. This bar

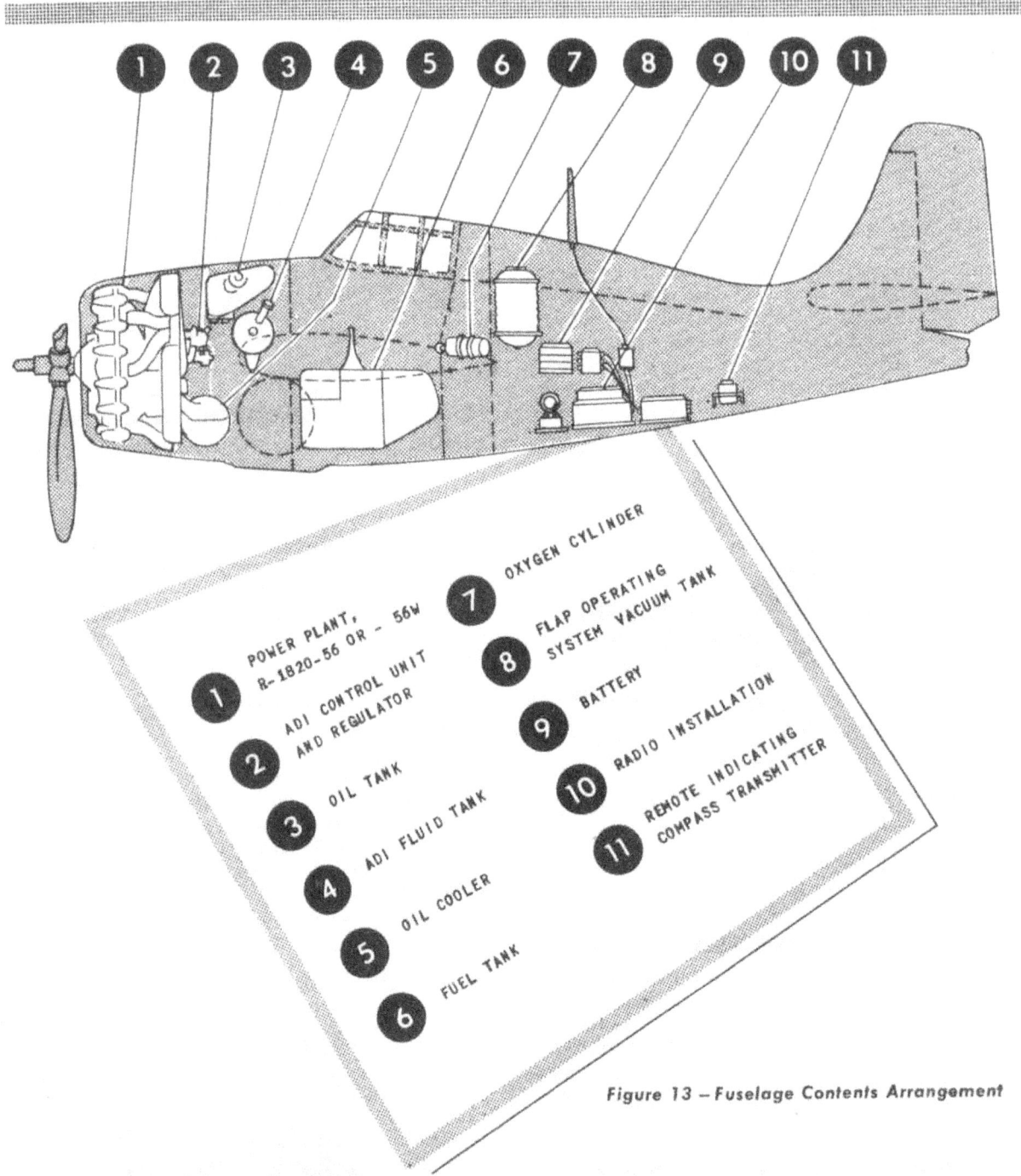

Figure 13 — Fuselage Contents Arrangement

takes up the extra loads during arrested landings which might otherwise crush the pilot's seat.

f. MAP CASE.—A canvas map case including a pad and pencil holder is installed on the left hand side of the cockpit above the shelf under the cockpit rail.

g. CHART BOARD.—The chart board is located directly beneath the main instrument panel. It may be pulled aft provided the clasp on the left hand corner is released. This clasp is installed to hold the board in place when the airplane is catapulted.

Section 2

NORMAL OPERATING INSTRUCTIONS

1. BEFORE ENTERING THE PILOT'S COMPARTMENT.

a. FLIGHT LIMITATIONS AND RESTRICTIONS.

(1) MANEUVERS PROHIBITED.

(a) No standard maneuvers are prohibited when operating without droppable fuel tanks. Catapulting, field landings, and arrested landings are permissible with 100-pound class bombs on the wing racks.

(b) When carrying one or more droppable tanks the following maneuvers are not permitted:

loops	Immelman turns
snap rolls	normal spins
chandelles	prolonged spins

When such tanks are carried the following maneuvers are permitted:

- wing overs
- vertical turns
- aileron rolls (only for entering a dive)
- inverted flight (only for entering a dive)

(2) PERMISSIBLE ACCELERATIONS

Gross Weight Pounds	Permissible Positive Acceleration
7700	7.5g*
7800	7.4g
8000	7.2g
8200	7.0g

*When carrying filled droppable fuel tanks the maximum permissible positive acceleration is 4.0g.

(3) LIMITING AIRSPEEDS.

(a) DIVING.—Terminal velocity dives are permissible with the airplane equipped as a fighter or as a bomber with two 100-pound class bombs on the wing racks. Speed with droppable tanks is unrestricted provided the tank and sway braces are correctly installed, i.e., the forward sway brace shank is in the sway brace wing socket as far as possible so that slight tank deformation will not allow the brace to drop out of the socket.

(b) WING FLAPS.—There is no limiting airspeed for lowering the wing flaps. Regardless of the position of the flap control valve, the flaps will not come down if the airspeed is in excess of 130 knots (150 MPH) as air pressure holds the flaps up until the air speed has dropped below that point.

(c) LANDING GEAR.—There is no limiting airspeed for lowering the landing gear. However, if the gear is lowered above the airspeed of 150 knots (172 MPH), air loads on the gear will cause the handcrank to whip free and spin rapidly.

NOTE

These limitations may be supplemented or superseded by instructions included in Service publications.

b. EFFECT OF INITIAL GROSS WEIGHT.
Before entering the airplane for any flight the pilot should obtain the initial gross weight of the airplane and then consult flight charts included herein to determine the characteristics of the airplane at the given loading condition. For example, the difference in loading between normal fighter and overload fighter will necessitate an additional take-off distance of approximately 100 feet in a 15 knot wind. Also radically affected by weight changes are the rate of climb, landing distance and service ceiling.

c. AIRPLANE ENTRY.
Entry into the airplane when the canopy is closed should be from the starboard side. A step and hand hole are provided on each side of the fuselage. To open a closed canopy, unfasten the small door marked *Enclosure Release* located just below the windshield on the starboard side. Reaching inside, rotate the canopy handle upward and push aft.

2. PRE-FLIGHT CHECK LISTS.

a. PILOT'S STANDARD CHECK LIST.

(1) Adjust the harness, making certain that the

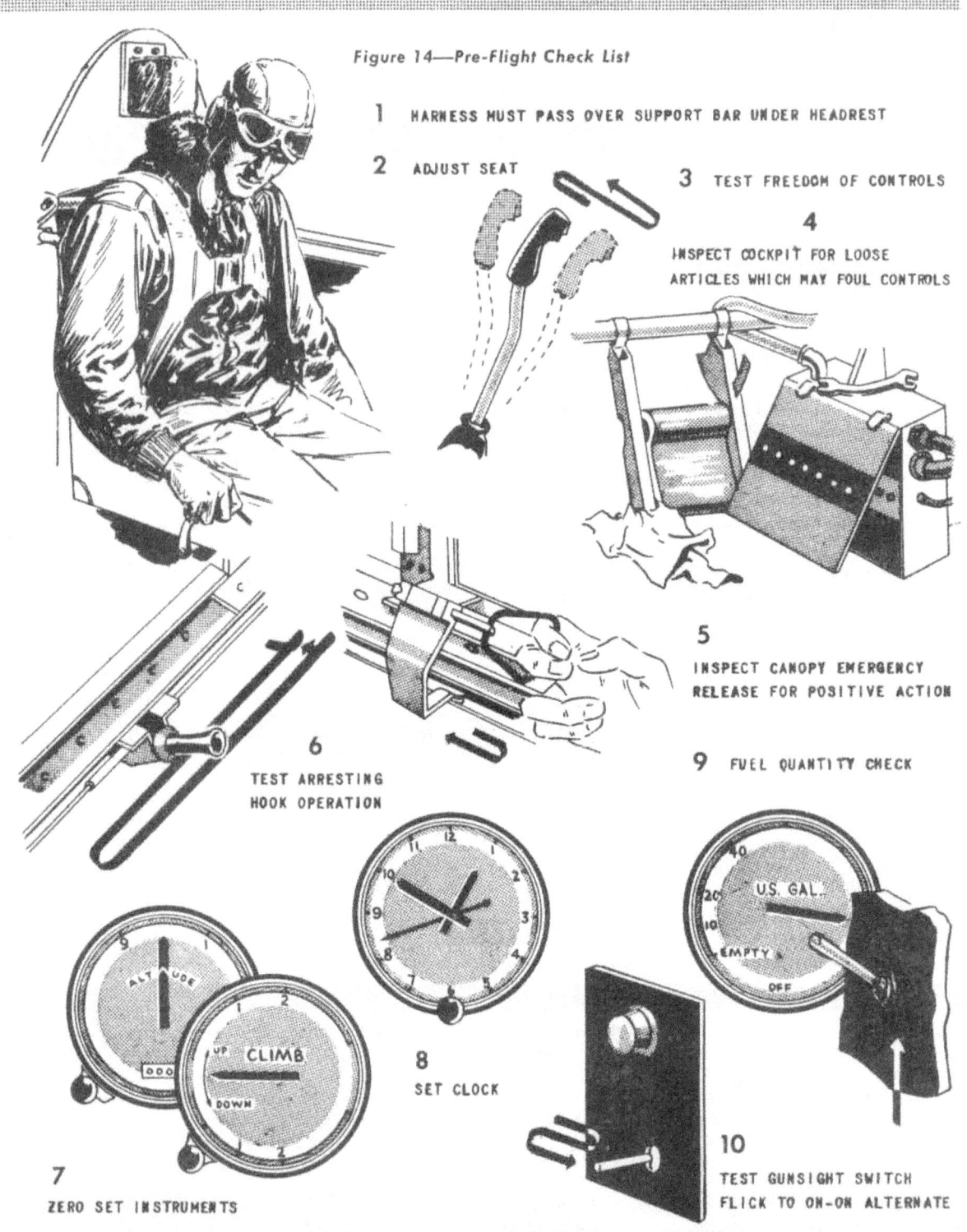

Figure 14—Pre-Flight Check List

shoulder harness passes over the support bar under the headrest.

(2) Adjust the seat to the desired level.

(3) Test controls for freedom of movement.

(4) Inspect cockpit for loose objects which may foul the controls.

(5) Check each wing for visible red flag which would indicate that the wing fold locking pin is not securely locked.

(6) Inspect the canopy emergency release pin to see that it is straight and lightly greased.

(7) Test the freedom of operation of the arresting hook by lowering and raising, making certain that it locks in the extended position.

(8) Uncage all instruments and check for zero settings. Test the setting knobs for freedom of movement.

NOTE

The gyro horizon and directional gyro indicators should be left uncaged at all times except during maneuvers in which the operating limits of the indicators would be exceeded. The operating limits are:

	Dive or Climb	Bank, Left or Right
Gyro Horizon Indicator	70°	100°
Directional Gyro Indicator	55°	55°

(9) Wind the clock and set it to the operations' office time.

(10) Turn on the battery switch and check fuel quantity on the gauge.

(11) If a pyrotechnic pistol is installed, inspect the shells for proper colors.

(12) Check the oxygen equipment as outlined in Section V, Paragraph 1c.

(13) Test the operation of the gun sight by turning on the battery switch and, with the rheostat turned up, flicking the gun sight switch from *On* to *On Alternate*. Make sure that both filaments are working.

THIS PAGE INTENTIONALLY LEFT BLANK.

(14) There is no test for quantity of ammunition other than a visual inspection of the ammunition boxes. However, gun loading can be checked by operating the gun charging handles until a loaded shell is ejected from the bottom of the wing. As this operation leaves a loaded shell in the gun chamber, take-off should be accomplished with the gun charging handles locked in safety position.

(15) Check the radio equipment as outlined in Section V, Paragraph 2e.

b. SPECIAL NIGHT CHECK LIST.

(1) Complete check list indicated above.

(2) With the battery switch on, turn up the rheostats to test the cockpit lights, instrument panel lights, compass light, and chartboard light.

(3) Test the section and formation lights by operating the switches.

(4) Have a ground crew member check the approach light operation when arresting gear test is made as outlined in Paragraph 2a(7).

(5) Check the operation of the recognition lights by use of toggle and keying switches.

3. FUEL SYSTEM MANAGEMENT.

Before starting a take-off, switch the fuel selector valve to the Main Tank using the emergency fuel pump to insure the proper system pressure. If droppable fuel tanks are carried, use about 15 gallons from the main tank to allow room for vapor return. Then switch to the droppable tanks, using that fuel first inasmuch as the tanks greatly increase drag and cause restrictions to be placed on maneuvers. When switching tanks, turn on the emergency fuel pump, move the selector switch to the proper tank, and check engine gauge unit for fuel pressure as the emergency fuel pump is turned off. If the pressure drops, turn on the emergency fuel pump again.

Fuel may be drawn from either droppable tank but the pilot should compensate by means of the trim tabs for the loss of weight on one wing as the fuel is used. Trim tab adjustment will compensate for a full tank on one wing and an empty tank on the other.

The emergency fuel pump is also used in case of failure of the engine driven pump or of lowered fuel pressure due to high altitudes.

Landing should always be attempted with fuel from the main tank and with the emergency fuel pump on.

4. FUNCTION OF THE MANIFOLD PRESSURE REGULATOR.

a. To obtain automatic regulation of manifold pressures necessary for ADI operation, a Delco Remy MP Regulator has been installed. This Regulator is adjusted by the pilot's throttle control lever. Movement of this lever selects the manifold pressure at which the pilot wishes to operate and sets that pressure on the Regulator. The Regulator then takes over to hold the selected manifold pressure through all conditions of flight within the critical altitude of that MP-RPM setting. As the airplane is climbed the Regulator opens the carburetor throttle as necessary to maintain the selected pressure until at the critical altitude for that operational setting the carburetor throttle is wide open. If the climb continues and RPM is held constant, the Regulator holds the throttle wide open. Further advance of the Throttle Control lever will have no effect as the carburetor throttle is already wide open.

NOTE

Preliminary calculations suggest that the linkage between the Regulator and the carburetor throttle will not permit Regulator to fully open the throttle when in lower MP ranges. Until definite information is available, the pilot may consider the Regulator as fully automatic at operation above 60% power. When operating below 60% power and manifold pressure starts to fall off, again move the throttle control lever forward to reselect the desired MP. The Regulator will then hold the selected pressure until the critical altitude for that MP-RPM setting is reached.

b. Movement of the supercharger control lever from Low Blower position to High Blower position automatically lowers the throttle selected manifold pressure about 4 inches Hg to values approximately consistent with engine calibration curves.

5. WAR EMERGENCY POWER.

a. A joggle in the throttle control quadrant rail marks the take-off and Military Power position of the throttle control. This joggle is adjustable to allow resetting of the take-off position. When the throttle control lever is against the stop and the RPM is 2600, the pilot obtains Military Power, using Low blower below 13000 feet or High blower above 13000 feet. Movement of the throttle control lever past the joggle stop to the full forward position allows an additional boost (War Emergency Power) to a maximum of 70 inches Hg in Low blower, 52 inches Hg in High blower while the anti-detonant fluid is flowing and 46 inches Hg manifold pressure in High blower when the fluid is exhausted.

b. The anti-detonant fluid will flow only in High blower at War Emergency Power. The manifold pressure regulator will permit a maximum of 52 inches Hg while the fluid is flowing and will automatically reset the manifold pressure to a maximum of 46 inches Hg when the fluid is exhausted. When the manifold pressure drops to 43 inches Hg in High blower the regulator will stop the flow of water.

WARNING

Continuous operation at War Emergency Power is limited to 5 minutes. Maximum cylinder head temperature is 248°C (478°F).

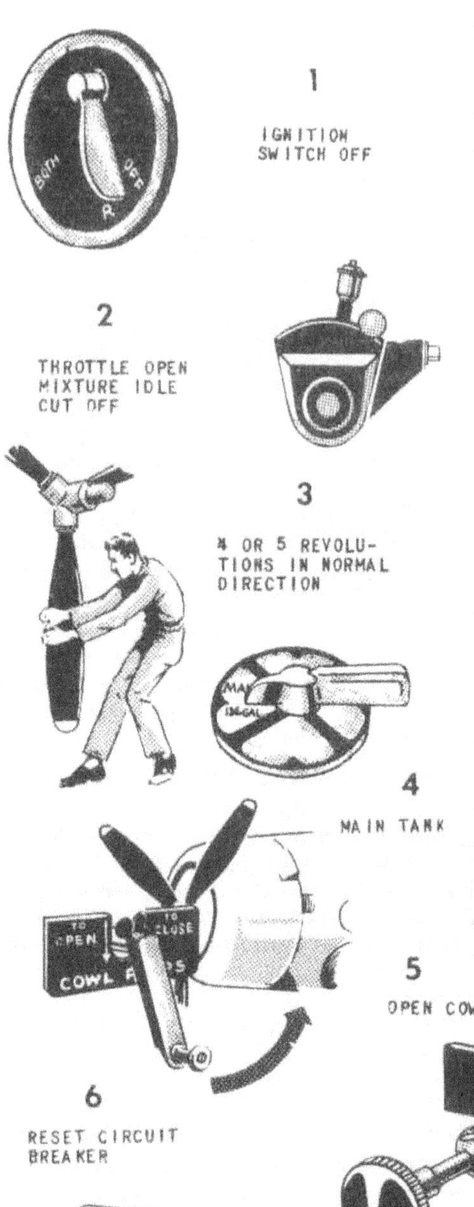

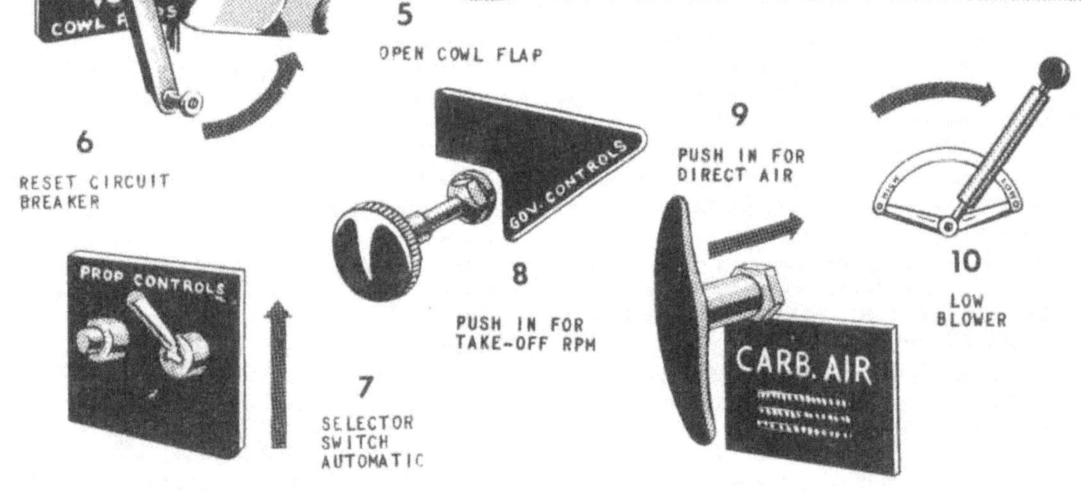

6. STARTING.

a. NORMAL STARTING CHECK-OFF LIST.

(1) Leave the ignition switch on *Off*.

(2) Set the mixture control in *Idle Cut-Off* position.

(3) Move the throttle full forward.

(4) Rotate the engine by hand for four or five revolutions in the normal direction. If an abnormal effort is required, remove the spark plugs from the lower cylinders to determine whether liquid has collected in the cylinder.

CAUTION

This installation has a tendency for oil to collect in the cylinders when engine is not operating. If engine is not pulled through by hand before starting, "liquid locks" with bent and broken lower link rods will result.

(5) Move the fuel selector valve handle to *Main Tank*.

(6) Fully open the cowl flaps.

(7) Push the propeller circuit breaker switch to insure that the circuit is closed.

(8) Snap the propeller selector switch into *Automatic* position.

(9) Push the propeller governor control knob full in for take-off RPM.

(10) Push the carburetor air control knob full in for *Direct Air* position.

(11) Lock the supercharger control in *Low* position.

(12) Insert a cartridge into the starter breech and lock the breech.

Figure 15—Starting Check List

(13) Set the throttle for 1000 RPM. *Do not pump or move the throttle abruptly until the engine is running smoothly.*

(14) Snap on the battery switch.

(15) Snap on the emergency fuel pump to build up a pressure of 14-16 PSI.

(16) Close the primer switch for three to five seconds immediately before firing the starter. The exact amount of priming will be varied as indicated by experience.

(17) Turn the ignition switch to *Both*.

(18) Snap the starter switch to fire the cartridge.

(19) Advance the mixture control to *Auto Rich* as the engine fires. If the engine stops immediately, return the mixture control to *Idle Cut-Off* position and switch off the emergency pump.

(20) Flick the primer switch intermittently until the engine runs smoothly.

(21) Idle the engine at 1000 RPM.

CAUTION

If in starting, oil pressure is not indicated in ten seconds, shut down the engine and investigate.

b. HARD STARTING.

(1) Follow the starting check-off list carefully. Wait a few minutes to allow any of the spilled fuel to drain out of the intake ducts and to permit the cartridge starter to cool before repeating the attempt.

(2) If it is suspected that the engine is over-primed, clear the cylinders and induction system of excess fuel by the following procedure:

  (a) Mixture Control..........................Idle Cut-Off

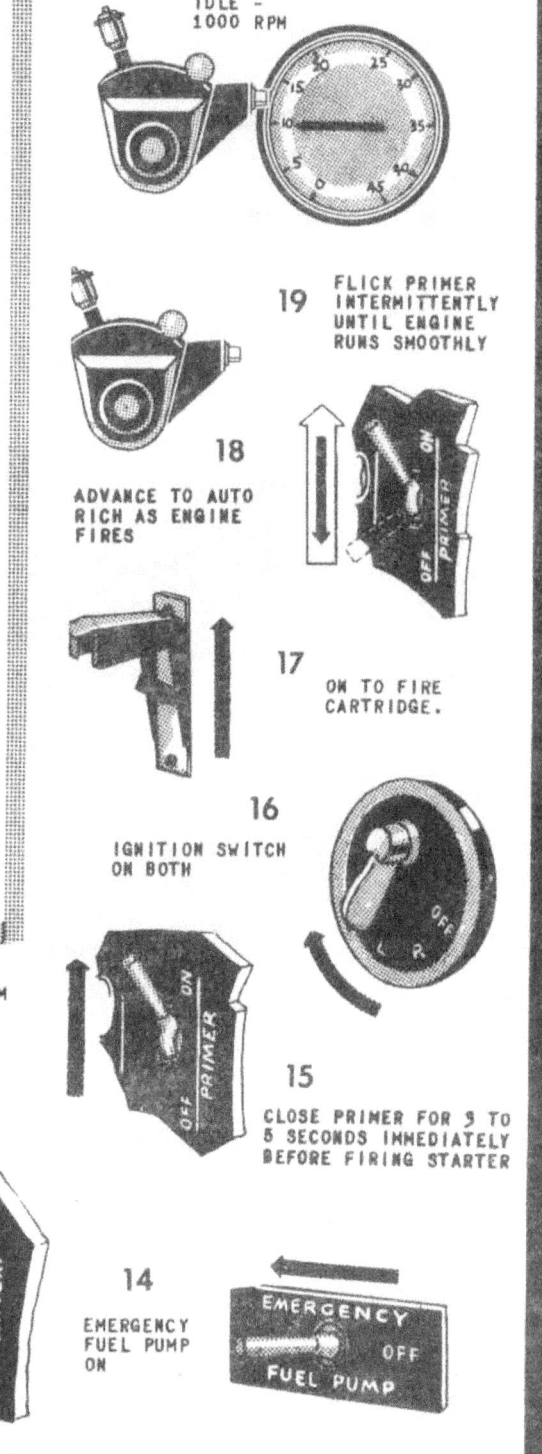

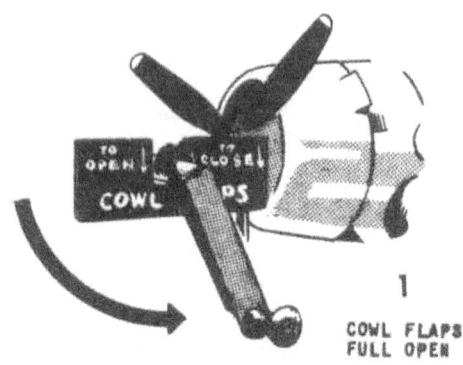

Figure 16—Warm-Up Check List

1. COWL FLAPS FULL OPEN

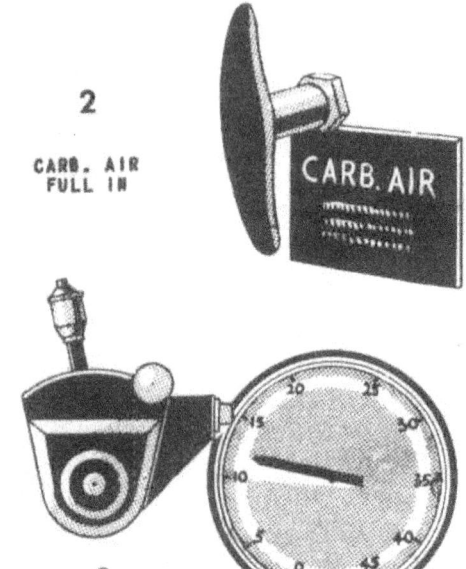

2. CARB. AIR FULL IN

3. THROTTLE FROM 1000 TO 1200 AS ENGINE RUNS SMOOTHLY

4. CHECK ENGINE GAUGE UNIT

(b) Auxiliary Fuel Pump .... Off
(c) Ignition Switch .... Off
(d) Throttle .... Full Open
(e) Rotate engine by hand ...... 4 or 5 revolutions

(3) If the propeller turns over but the engine fails to start, do not fire more than three cartridges consecutively without allowing a period of at least five minutes for starter parts to cool. If the starting attempt fails to result in the normal rotation of the propeller, another cartridge should not be fired until the trouble has been determined and corrected. In the event of a safety disc failure, turn the engine propeller by hand to determine whether the engine is free. If the cartridge should fail to fire, do not remove the cartridge from the breech for at least five minutes.

NOTE

In all circumstances Type C cartridges should be used.

(4) After starting, if heavy viscous oil is indicated by oil pressure that is too high, fluctuates, or falls off when engine RPM is increased, the dilution valve may be operated intermittently (not continuously) to correct the condition. This is not considered good practice and should be used only in emergency. Allow adequate warm-up before taking off with diluted oil except in cases of extreme emergency.

c. EMERGENCY OPERATION OF CARTRIDGE STARTERS.—If the cartridge starter fails to fire because of an open circuit, the following emergency method can be used: Connect two flashlight batteries to a brass prod and a battery clamp. Insert a momentary contact toggle switch in the circuit between the batteries and the brass prod. Ground the battery clamp to the fuselage. Insert the prod directly against the electric contact strip in the lower part of the cartridge starter breech completing the circuit by closing the switch. This will fire the cartridge. Other controls are operated as in the normal starting procedure outlined above.

d. IN CASE OF FIRE.

(1) The pilot should visually check to ascertain that a member of the ground crew is on duty off his wing tip with a fire bottle before starting the engine.

(2) If an engine fire breaks out while starting, turn the fuel selector valve *Off*, switch the emergency fuel pump *Off*, increase the throttle setting but keep the ignition switch *On* until the propeller has stopped turning. This will suck any fuel and fire in the lines, ducts and carburetor into the engine where the fuel will be ignited, partially dissipated and passed out through the exhaust with the flames. If the fire continues or shows any signs of spreading the fire bottle should be employed by the ground crew.

7. GROUND CHECK.

a. WARM-UP.

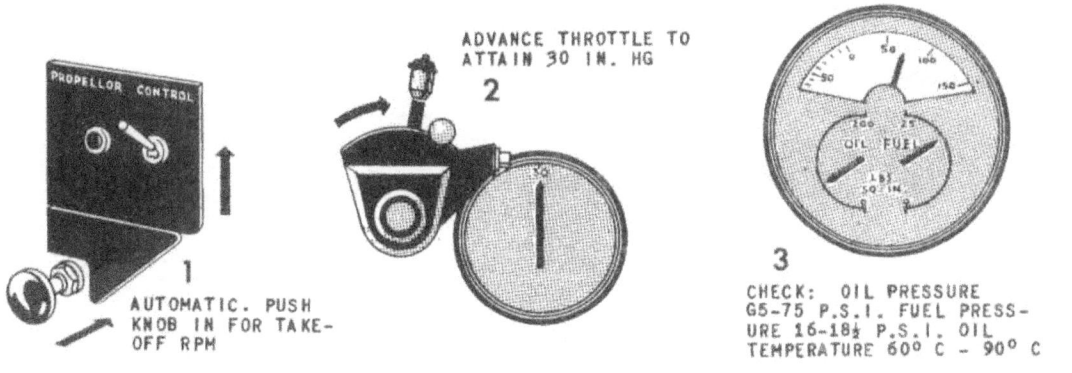

Figure 17—Engine Operation Check

(1) Fully open the cowl flaps.

(2) An oil pressure of 65-75 PSI is desired. If excessive pressure is obtained in cold weather, operate at 800 RPM until the oil pressure drops to the desired range.

(3) Push carburetor air control full in for *Direct* position.

(4) Idle the engine at 1000 RPM.

(5) When the engine fires smoothly, gradually open the throttle to 1200 RPM and run it at this speed until the oil inlet temperature reaches a minimum of 30°C (86°F).

b. ENGINE CHECK.

(1) Open the throttle to 30 in Hg. with propeller set for take-off RPM.

(2) The oil pressure should maintain 65-75 PSI. If the oil pressure drops or fluctuates when the throttle is open, reduce speed and continue with the warm-up procedure.

c. MAGNETO CHECK.

(1) Set the propeller in "Automatic" for take-off RPM and set throttle for a manifold pressure reading of 30 in Hg.

(2) Move the magneto switch from *Both to Left*. The tachometer should show a drop of less than 100 RPM.

(3) Move the magneto switch from *Left to Both*. Wait until RPM stabilizes and move switch to Right. The tachometer should again show a drop of less than 100 RPM.

d. CARBURETOR IDLE MIXTURE CHECK.—Make idle mixture check with throttle set for 600 RPM and auxiliary fuel pump "ON". Move the mixture control lever smoothly and steadily into the *IDLE CUT-OFF* position and observe the tachometer for any change in RPM. Return the mixture control lever to *AUTO-RICH* position before the engine cuts out. The smallest noticeable rise in RPM during the check indicates a

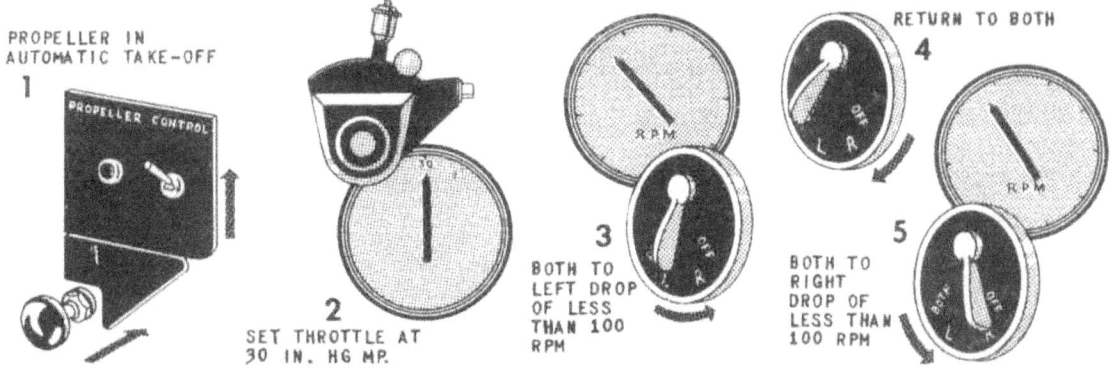

Figure 18—Magneto Operation Check

Figure 19—Manifold Pressure Regulator Check

satisfactory idle mixture adjustment, in order to permit idling at low speeds without danger of fouling plugs and at the same time to afford good acceleration characteristics. A rise in excess of 50 RPM indicates too rich a mixture. No rise or a drop in RPM indicates too lean a mixture.

e. MANIFOLD PRESSURE REGULATOR CHECK.

(1) With the propeller controls in the Take-Off position, open the throttle gradually to obtain 30 inches Hg manifold pressure. During this operation the RPM should climb steadily without lag or irregularities.

(2) Pull propeller governor control back to obtain 1700 RPM without changing the throttle and shift to high blower. A manifold pressure drop of 4 inches Hg should result. After the manifold pressure has stabilized return to low blower and note return of manifold pressure to 30 inches Hg.

(3) Return propeller governor control to Take-Off position and retard throttle to warm-up RPM.

f. PROPELLER OPERATION CHECK.

(1) MANUAL.

(*a*) Propeller circuit breaker "ON."

(*b*) Set Propeller selector switch in "Fixed Pitch."

(*c*) Hold selector switch in *Increase RPM* until a gain in RPM is noted on the tachometer then release switch (Return to *Fixed Pitch*).

(*d*) Hold selector switch in *Decrease RPM* until a drop in RPM is noted on the tachometer then release switch (Return to *Fixed Pitch*).

(2) AUTOMATIC.

(*a*) Set propeller selector switch in *Automatic*. Push propeller governor control knob all the way in for take-off (2600) RPM.

(*b*) Set throttle to obtain 1800 RPM.

(*c*) Pull out the propeller governor control knob until a decrease of approximately 200 RPM is obtained. A steady speed without surging should result.

(*d*) Return the propeller governor control knob to take-off RPM (full in). The original RPM (1800) should again be attained showing that the propeller is operating correctly in *Automatic*.

NOTE

With the Curtiss Electric Propeller, an adequate supply of electrical energy for *Automatic* control of propeller is essential for a safe take-off and operation in flight. Pilots should therefore form the habit of checking the ammeter during ground checks for an indication of current flow from the generator. The engine speed should be well above 1100 to 1300 RPM at which speed the generator cuts out when this check is made. If the generator is not supplying current to the electrical system, the reserve electrical energy of the battery is all that is available. To attempt a take-off and flight under these conditions may be disastrous.

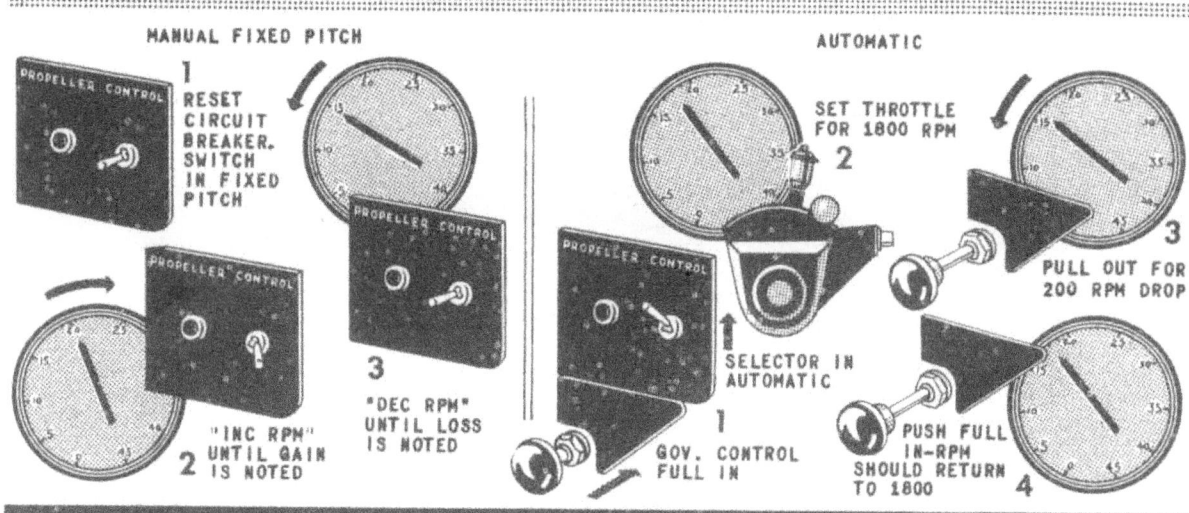

Figure 20—Propeller Operation Check

g. SUPERCHARGER DESLUDGING OPERATION.—Desludge supercharger by operating in each blower position for 30 seconds at about 100 RPM.

h. SUPERCHARGER CHECK.—Whenever it is desired to check the operation of the supercharger proceed as follows:

(1) With the propeller controls in the Take-off position open throttle to obtain 1700 RPM.

(2) Shift to high blower and open throttle further to obtain 30 inches Hg and note RPM.

(3) Close throttle completely. Shift to low blower and open throttle to 30 inches Hg again.

(4) If RPM is appreciably higher now than with 30 inches Hg in high blower the check is satisfactory.

8. EMERGENCY TAKE-OFF.

Emergency take-offs without full warm-up are not recommended. The engine has a tendency to run cool and to cool even further while taxiing. In an emergency, take-off may be made when oil-in temperature is 20°C (68°F) and oil pressure remains steady after opening the throttle.

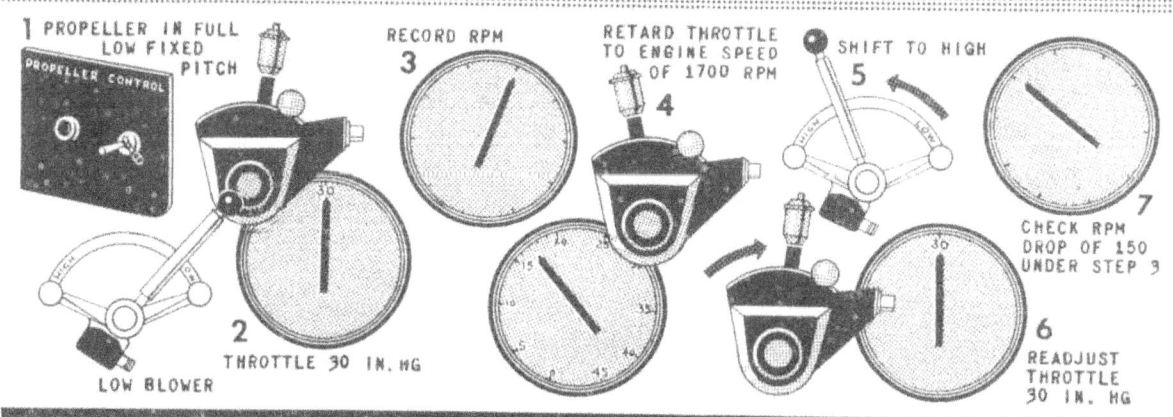

Figure 21—Supercharger Check

Section II

RESTRICTED
AN 01-190FB-1

Figure 22—Take-Off Check List

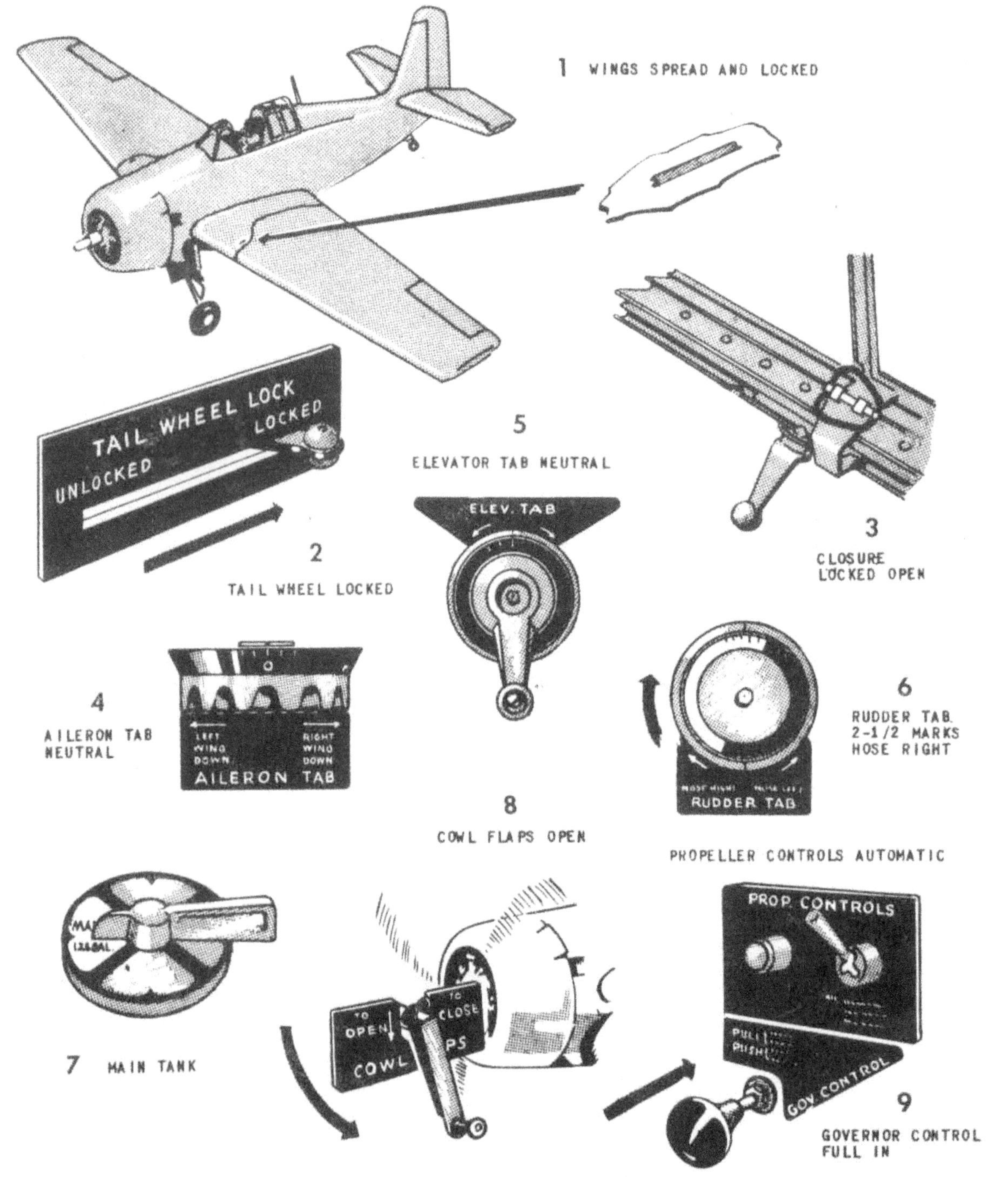

1 WINGS SPREAD AND LOCKED

2 TAIL WHEEL LOCKED

3 CLOSURE LOCKED OPEN

4 AILERON TAB NEUTRAL

5 ELEVATOR TAB NEUTRAL

6 RUDDER TAB. 2-1/2 MARKS NOSE RIGHT

7 MAIN TANK

8 COWL FLAPS OPEN

PROPELLER CONTROLS AUTOMATIC

9 GOVERNOR CONTROL FULL IN

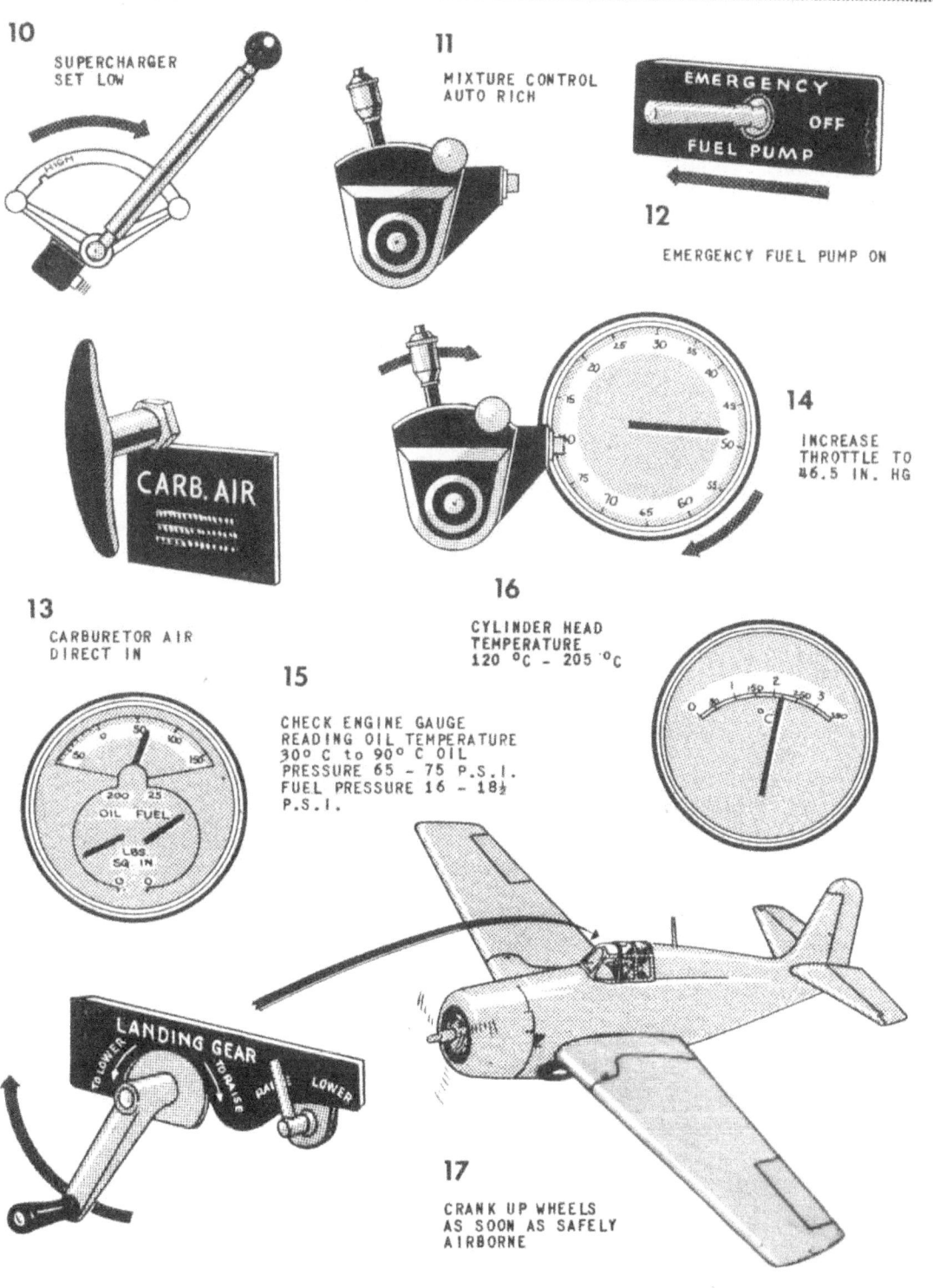

9. TAXIING INSTRUCTIONS.

No unusual characteristics exist. Turns of 360° in either direction may be made with ease. Brakes should be carefully applied as, the airplane has a tendency to nose over when the brakes are *jammed on*.

In all taxiing operations caution should be exercised to insure that the tail wheel is unlocked whether the plane is handled by a tractor or under its own power. The tail wheel locking pin may be sheared off otherwise.

As the engine cools during taxiing, further warm-up is usually required to bring the cylinder head temperature above minimum before entering the take-off run.

10. TAKE-OFF.

a. DISCUSSION.—*Before starting the take-off run see that the oil temperatures are above the low limits and not near the upper limits.*

Oil-in Temperature............30°C (86°F) Minimum
20°C (68°F) Emergency

Oil Pressure....................................65-75 PSI

Fuel Pressure
(With emergency pump on) 16-18½ PSI

For a rolling start, open the throttle gradually until a maximum of 46.5 in. Hg is obtained. The airplane will *take itself off* from a three-point position at about 70 to 75 knots.

In a standing start, gradually release the brakes when the manifold pressure reaches about 25 in. Hg. If the brakes are held, the tail begins to jump at about 30 in. Hg.

If it should be necessary to take-off in a cross wind make every attempt to keep the wind from the left. Adjust the rudder tab right in accordance with the strength of the cross wind.

CAUTION

Regardless of the altitude of the airport always take-off in low blower.

b. EXPANDED TAKE-OFF CHECK LIST.

(1) Visually check signal flags in wing to be certain that wings are spread and locked.

(2) Lock the tail wheel.

(3) Lock the cockpit enclosure in *Full Open* position.

(4) Set the aileron tab in neutral.

(5) Set the elevator tab in neutral.

(6) Set the rudder tab control at 2½ units nose right.

(7) Switch the fuel tank selector valve to *Main*.

(8) Open the cowl flaps.

(9) Set the propeller selector switch in *Automatic* with the push-pull knob full in for 2600 RPM (Take-off RPM).

(10) Set supercharger control in *Low*.

(11) Set the mixture control in *Auto Rich*.

(12) Flick on the emergency fuel pump.

(13) Move the carburetor air control to *Direct*.

(14) Advance the throttle to the take-off joggle to obtain 46.5 in. Hg manifold pressure.

CAUTION

Do not move the throttle control lever beyond the Take-off stop. The exact position of the stop should be adjusted to conform to the Take-off Power determined for the operational area.

11. ENGINE FAILURE DURING TAKE-OFF.

To provide greater safety in the event of a forced landing due to power failure, retract the landing gear as soon as the airplane is safely airborne.

NOTE

On take-off the landing gear should be brought up immediately as high air loads caused by increasing speed make the cranking operation much more difficult.

To come in for a landing without power from very low altitude, lock the tail wheel, cut the ignition, put the airplane's nose down to start a glide and prevent stall. Then bring the nose up until the airplane is approximately the same attitude as for a normal landing, allowing the tail wheel to touch first and act as a drag.

WARNING

With power off or with low power this ship is excessively nose heavy and, in the event of an engine failure, will stall if a fairly good gliding angle is not immediately assumed.

12. CLIMB.

a. DISCUSSION.—The best climbing airspeed for this airplane is about 125 knots indicated. Speeds slightly higher than this have very little effect on the rate of climb but result in better cooling. At these relatively low speeds it should be noted that the resulting reduction in Ram brings about a lower airplane critical altitude. If after increasing airspeed, cooling is not improved, the cowl flaps must be adjusted to hold the temperature within the specified limits.

NOTE

Above 20,500 ft. altitude do not exceed 2500 RPM. The use of 2600 RPM above this altitude results in a loss of propeller efficiency. The thrust, and consequently the airspeed, will be improved at 2500 RPM and the fuel consumption will be less than at 2600 RPM.

b. RATED POWER CLIMB.—Operate according to the Power Plant Chart and the Engine Calibration Curve. The following table shows the throttle and supercharger settings for this condition.

TABLE I

PRESS. ALT. (No Ram)	MAN. PRESS., IN. HG.	BLOWER RATIO
S.L. —5700	43— Full Throttle	Low
5700 —14000	Full Throttle	Low
14000—20700	38— Full Throttle	High
20700—Up	Full Throttle	High

Cylinder Head Temperature of 218°C (424°F) can be maintained continuously or temperature up to 232°C (450°F) for one hour.

c. MILITARY POWER CLIMB.—Operate in accordance with the Power Plant Charts and Engine Calibration Curve. The following table gives the throttle and supercharger settings for this condition:

TABLE II

PRESS. ALT. (No Ram)	MAN. PRESS., IN. HG.	BLOWER RATIO
S.L. —3500	46.5— Full Throttle	Low
3500 —13000	Full Throttle	Low
13000—17800	43— Full Throttle	High
17800—Up	Full Throttle	High

Cylinder Head Temperature of 232°C (450°F) can be maintained for 30 minutes.

d. WAR EMERGENCY POWER CLIMB— The use of WEP in climb in low blower below 1000 feet gives very little advantage over climb with military power at the same altitude. While the following table gives the throttle and supercharger settings for a WEP climb it also shows the effect of Ram as discussed in paragraph *a* on the airplane critical altitudes by giving the airplane critical altitudes while climbing and in level flight. The ADI system (high blower) may be operated with definite gain in power between approximately 6,500 feet (where the manifold pressure drops to 42 inches Hg in low blower) and 17,800 feet (where the manifold pressure drops to 43 inches Hg in high blower.)

TABLE III

BLOWER RATIO	MAP AT FULL THROTTLE	CRITICAL ALTITUDE CLIMB	CRITICAL ALTITUDE LEVEL FLIGHT
Low	50	-1200	1200
High	52 (Wet)	7800	10800
High	46 (dry)	11800	14400

Cylinder Head Temperature of 248°C (478°F) can be maintained for 5 minutes.

For maximum performance shift blowers at the altitude where the manifold pressure is 42 inches Hg.

13. GENERAL FLYING CHARACTERISTICS.

a. CRUISING BELOW NORMAL RATED POWER.—The mixture control should be in *Auto Lean* for the cruising power operation as shown in the Engine Calibration Curve. If the head temperature cannot be kept below 205°C (401°F) with cowl flaps open, the mixture should be enriched.

The cruising manifold pressure-RPM relationships specified in the Engine Calibration Curve should not be exceeded.

Cruising operations can be carried on at any power below Normal Rated Power. The best fuel economy is realized at powers below Maximum Cruise.

Use the Flight Operating Instructions Chart to determine recommended cruising conditions based on fuel quantity and rate of consumption. Engine settings for cruising conditions are condensed in the Power Plant Chart.

b. CHANGING POWER CONDITIONS.

(1) TO INCREASE POWER.

(a) Set the desired RPM with the propeller governor control.

(b) Then adjust the throttle to obtain desired manifold pressure.

(2) TO DECREASE POWER.

(a) Set the desired manifold pressure with the throttle.

(b) Then set the desired RPM with the propeller governor. Readjust the throttle, if necessary.

c. SUPERCHARGER OPERATION.

(1) The Supercharger high blower should be used above 14,000 feet pressure-altitude for normal rated and lower powers. The high blower should not be used for cruising at altitude at which cruising power is available in low blower since greater fuel economy is obtainable in low rates.

(2) Shift from low to high blower as follows:

(a) Close the throttle as necessary to avoid exceeding the desired manifold pressure after shifting. Set the mixture control in *Auto Rich* to prevent engine from cutting out. Emergency fuel pump *On*.

NOTE

On those airplanes equipped with the Anti-Detonant Injection system the above step is not necessary to avoid exceeding the desired manifold pressure after shifting as the manifold pressure regulator will automatically reduce the throttle setting. If, however, the throttle setting is in the higher brackets it should be retarded to approximately 50% to 60% throttle to avoid shifting at high powers.

(b) Adjust the Propeller governor to attain 1700-1800 RPM (whenever possible). If many shifts are made above 1800 RPM or if any are made above 2500 RPM, failure of the supercharger clutch or drive may result.

(c) Shift rapidly from *Low* to *High* and lock in that position.

(d) Readjust throttle and propeller governor control for desired manifold pressure and RPM as necessary.

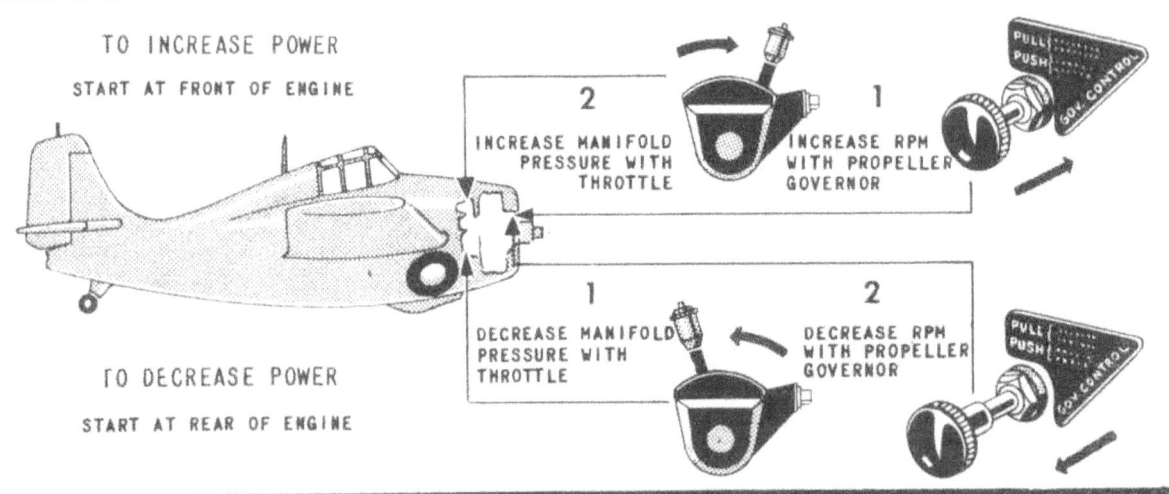

Figure 23—Changing Power

(e) Return the mixture control to *Auto-Lean*. Turn the emergency pump *OFF*.

(3) Shift from *High* to *Low* blower as follows:

(a) Retard throttle setting to 50% to 60% throttle.

(b) Adjust propeller governor control to attain 1500 RPM.

(c) Shift rapidly from *High* to *Low* and lock in that position.

(d) Readjust throttle and propeller governor control for desired manifold pressure and RPM as necessary.

(4) Except in an emergency, do not shift more often than at five minute intervals while in flight in order to provide sufficient time for the dissipation of heat generated during the clutch engagement period. This restriction need not be observed during checking operations on the ground because of low clutch loads imposed at low engine RPM.

(5) This engine uses a roller type clutch. A shift to high blower for a thirty second period during the warm-up prior to each day's flight at about 1000 RPM should be made to loosen any small accumulation of sludge and dirt about the clutch. To more completely desludge the clutch, all land based airplanes should be taxied to the line at 1000 RPM with the blower in *High* ratio for thirty seconds or more after each flight.

d. STABILITY.—The trim tabs have sufficient range to maintain stability. After initial flight the fixed tab on the right aileron can be set to compensate for wing heaviness.

e. MANEUVERS WITH MANIFOLD PRESSURE REGULATOR.—During the slow rolls or entrance into dives or *any maneuver producing a negative acceleration* the resulting loss of oil pressure in the manifold pressure regulator on those airplanes equipped with the

Anti Detonant Injection system (R-1820-56W engine) causes a drop in manifold pressure. The amount of drop increases as the critical altitude for the particular engine operating condition is approached attaining a magnitude that will almost cause the engine to cut out.

(1) This can be overcome by increasing the throttle setting as desired before going into any maneuver producing a negative acceleration. The throttle setting *must,* however, be returned to the original setting as the negative acceleration drops off (in most cases as the maneuver is completed) or a terrific surge of power will result.

(2) Due to the above condition, it is, therefore, recommended that except during conditions where the original power is definitely required during the maneuver, the original throttle setting be retained and the power be allowed to drop off temporarily.

WARNING

If icing conditions are suspected on those airplanes incorporating a Manifold Pressure Regulator, switch immediately to alternate air. As the carburetor starts to ice the Regulator will automatically open the carburetor throttle to compensate for loss of manifold pressure. Therefore, the pilot receives no warning until the carburetor has heavily iced.

f. OPERATION OF ADI SYSTEM FOR FAMILIARIZATION.—War Emergency Power is authorized only in combat areas. However, general operation of the equipment is permitted at altitudes above which full war emergency power may not be realized. Therefore, the following procedure is recommended to operate the ADI equipment for familiarization or operation outside combat areas.

(1) Climb to a pressure altitude of 16,750 feet or slightly higher (a minimum of the high blower military power critical altitude minus 1,000 feet) and level off.

(2) Attain a minimum of 43 inches of Hg without exceeding the take-off throttle stop as the ADI Control Unit will start to function at this MAP.

(3) Move the throttle lever to full boost position This will actuate the micro-switch on the throttle quadrant, completing the circuit to initiate ADI fluid injection (assuming the supercharger control is in *High* blower).

NOTE

There will be a slight increase in manifold pressure although full WEP manifold pressure will not be obtained as the altitude is above the "Wet" War Emergency Power critical altitude. Full WEP can be realized only at lower altitudes.

14. STALLS.

Stalls are fairly gentle with ample warning in clean, flapped or landing conditions. Warning appears as a shudder in the airplane just previous to the development of the full stall.

Stalling Speeds:	
Clean with power	68.5 knots
Flaps with power	61.0 knots
Landing condition with power	59.0 knots

Figure 24—Supercharger Operation

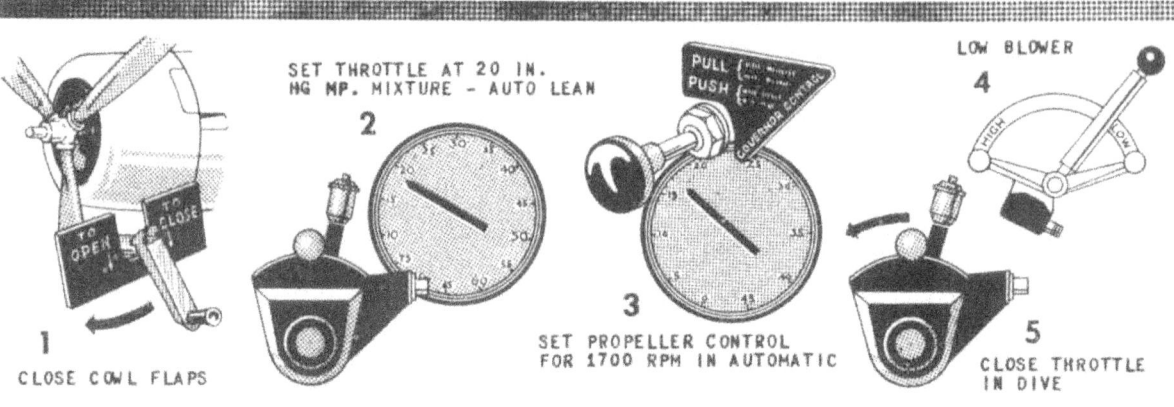

Figure 25—Diving Check List

Clean without power	74.5 knots
Flaps without power	67.0 knots
Landing condition without power	65.0 knots

The airplane tends to drop one wing or the other rather than mush after stall develops.

Aileron control is considered adequate at speeds five knots above stalling speed but not at the stall. The rudder, of course, may be used to raise a low wing after the ailerons become ineffective.

15. SPINS.

Recovery from normal fully developed spins to the left or right may be effected in $1\frac{1}{2}$ to 2 turns by the application of full opposite rudder and forward stick.

Right spins have an erratic tendency at times and will eventually become normal; however, during the first five or six turns of the abnormal spin, recovery is difficult and requires approximately four turns. If the abnormal spin is allowed to continue it will become normal after five or six turns and recovery can be affected in two turns.

Inverted spins are normal and recovery is easy.

In the landing condition the airplane has a tendency to start its rotation gently and then after about one third of a turn whip into the spin. The spin is gentle enough but has this peculiar whip in the early stages of the rotation.

16. PERMISSIBLE ACROBATICS.

All the usual military maneuvers are permitted except when carrying one or more droppable fuel tanks. When such tanks are carried, wing overs, aileron rolls and vertical turns are permitted; inverted flight is permitted only for entering a dive.

17. DIVING.

a. DISCUSSION.—Stick forces in dives not approaching a zero-lift dive are slightly aft, i.e. requiring a slight forward force. In a zero-lift dive there are no stick forces, i.e. the airplane tends to remain in the same attitude. The engine shall not be allowed to turn over 3100 RPM and the manifold pressure shall be kept below the limit for RPM and altitude. If the engine RPM does exceed 3100, close the throttle, shift the propeller to manual and full decrease RPM, and reduce the airspeed to the minimum speed for a safe glide.

During the dive the airplane has a tendency to droop the left wing and nose right. Correct this with the aileron tab and slight rudder pressure. This tendency increases as the diving speed increases and tab changes must be made accordingly. As the airplane comes out of the dive these tendencies drop off and trim should again be changed accordingly.

NOTE

If a high speed dive is anticipated, it is recommended that any tendencies the airplane may have to assume other attitudes than those desired be corrected with the stick and rudder pedals. This should be done in lieu of use of the trim tabs as slight changes in the angle of the tabs would cause noticeable results on the ship's attitude and subject the trim tabs to high structural loads.

The terminal velocity of this airplane is approximately 370 knots indicated at 15000 feet altitude and 7200 pounds gross weight. To recover from a terminal velocity dive a stick force of 75 to 100 pounds is required. There will also be a slight time lag between the application of the stick forces and the resulting change in the airplane's attitude.

b. EXPANDED DIVING CHECK-OFF LIST.

(1) Close the cowl flaps.

(2) Set throttle to attain 15 inches Hg with mixture control in "Auto-Lean."

NOTE

Any manifold pressure from 15 inches up to the maximum limiting manifold pressure for the RPM and altitude may be used. Any manifold pressure below 15 inches, if held in a prolonged dive, will foul up the engine in the same manner as do prolonged glides with a closed throttle. Care should be taken, however, not to let the manifold pressure build up over the limits as altitude is lost. THE GREATER THE MANIFOLD PRESSURE USED, THE GREATER WILL BE THE DIVING SPEED.

(3) Set propeller control in "Automatic" at 2100 RPM.

(4) Lock the supercharger in "Low" blower.

(5) Retard throttle setting during dive in accordance with above note.

18. NIGHT FLYING. (No Special Instructions)

19. APPROACH AND LANDING.

a. EXPANDED LANDING CHECK-OFF LIST.

(1) Crank the landing gear down.

(2) Lock the tail wheel caster for land operation. Unlock it for carrier operation.

(3) Lower and lock the arresting hook in position for carrier landing. Leave the hook up for normal landing.

(4) Open and lock the cockpit enclosure.

(5) Set the carburetor air control full in for *Direct* position.

(6) Set the propeller governor control for 2100 RPM.

NOTE

An approach speed of 85 knots is recommended. In slower approaches, the airplane has a tendency to nose down and lose stick control.

(7) Lock the supercharger in *Low* regardless of the airport altitude.

(8) Move the mixture control into *Auto Rich*.

(9) Close the cowl flaps for a normal land approach. Open the cowl flaps for a *power on* carrier approach only as necessary to maintain recommended cylinder head temperatures.

(10) Lower the wing flaps.

(11) Move the propeller governor control full "IN" just prior to landing.

(12) Open the cowl flaps wide just after landing.

NOTE

When lowering the landing flaps on this airplane the engine may "cough" and lose as much as 200 RPM during the operation. This drop is *normal and only temporary*. It is caused by a change in the mixture as the flaps are vacuum operated, the vacuum being created by the low pressure area in the carburetor venturi as shown in figure 3 and explained in Section I, paragraph 4.

b. CROSS WIND LANDING.—Follow the normal check-off list. Maintain a steep glide path to a position as close to the ground as possible. Do not attempt to hold the airplane off the ground any length of time. Allow the tail wheel to touch first with the caster locked. These instructions apply to cross wind or gusty conditions when holding off may give the wind a chance to pick up a wing while lateral control is sluggish.

c. WAVE-OFF CONDITION.—Power suddenly applied tends to raise the nose. Therefore, care should be exercised to push the stick forward or to use the nose-down tab when suddenly applying power in a *Wave-Off*. If this is not done a stall may develop.

Do not change flap settings. The flaps are forced up by the air stream as speed increases.

20. STOPPING THE ENGINE.

a. EXPANDED PILOT'S CHECK-OFF LIST.

(1) Leave the cowl flaps fully open while idling and for at least ten minutes after stopping.

(2) Leave the carburetor air control knob in for *Direct* position.

(3) Set the propeller control knob full in for Take-Off RPM.

(4) Leave the supercharger control in *Low*.

(5) Leave the mixture control in *Auto Rich*.

(6) Set the throttle for 800-1000 RPM to cool engine, and idle until head temperature drops below the desired 200°C (392°F) before stopping the engine.

It is desirable to shift the blower control at least once while operating at this RPM. (High Blower will not engage but the driving mechanism will be flushed.)

(7) When engine has cooled sufficiently, increase the speed to 1000-1200 RPM for one-half minute to scavenge.

(8) Move the mixture control to *Idle Cut-Off*.

(9) When the propeller stops rotating, shut off the ignition switch.

(10) Snap off the battery switch.

(11) Turn Fuel Selector Switch to *Off*.

b. OIL DILUTION PROCEDURE.

(1) In the event that temperatures below —5°C (23°F) are forecast for the period before the next start,

Section II
RESTRICTED
AN 01-190FB-1

Figure 26—Approach and Landing Check List

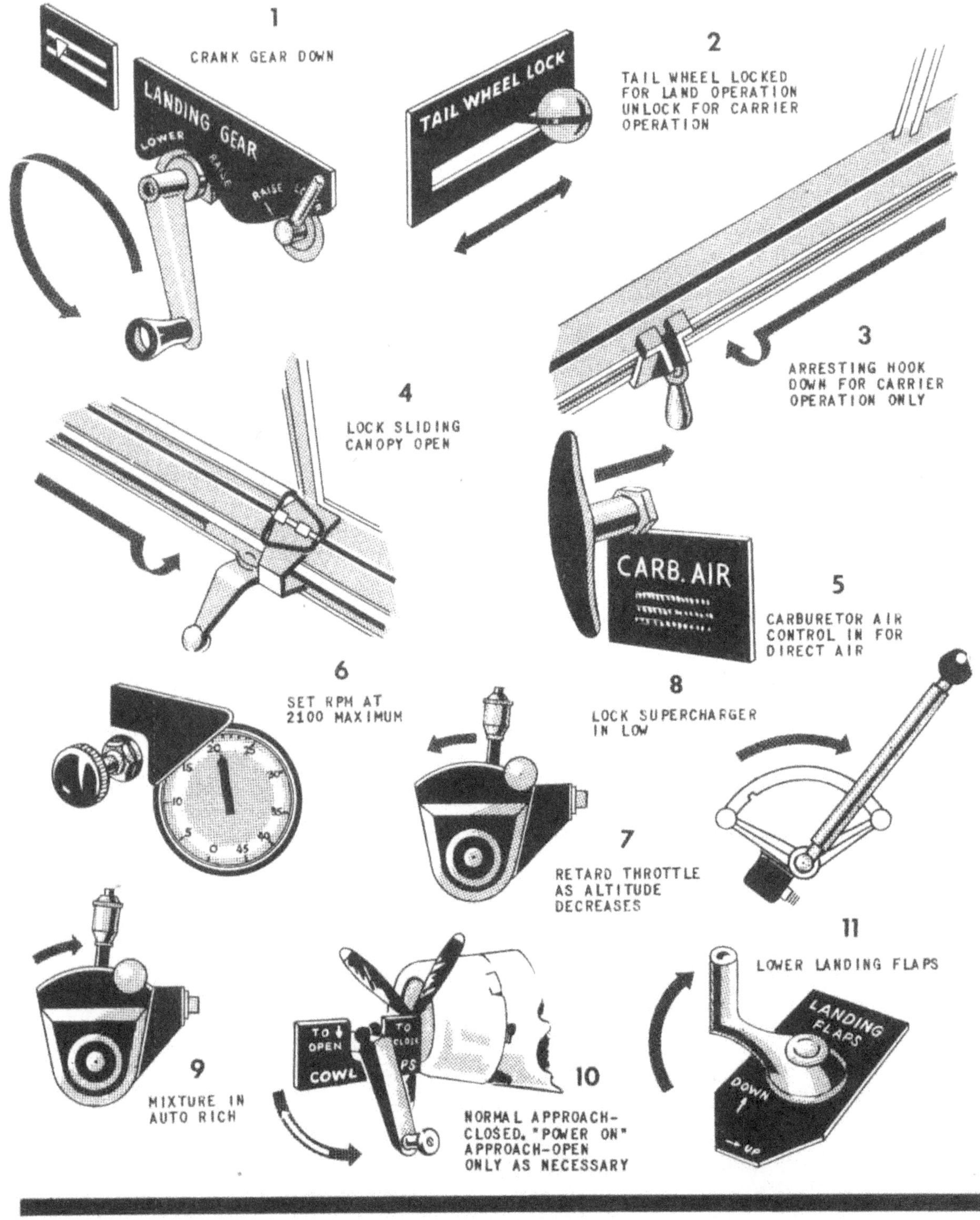

1. CRANK GEAR DOWN
2. TAIL WHEEL LOCKED FOR LAND OPERATION UNLOCK FOR CARRIER OPERATION
3. ARRESTING HOOK DOWN FOR CARRIER OPERATION ONLY
4. LOCK SLIDING CANOPY OPEN
5. CARBURETOR AIR CONTROL IN FOR DIRECT AIR
6. SET RPM AT 2100 MAXIMUM
7. RETARD THROTTLE AS ALTITUDE DECREASES
8. LOCK SUPERCHARGER IN LOW
9. MIXTURE IN AUTO RICH
10. NORMAL APPROACH—CLOSED. "POWER ON" APPROACH—OPEN ONLY AS NECESSARY
11. LOWER LANDING FLAPS

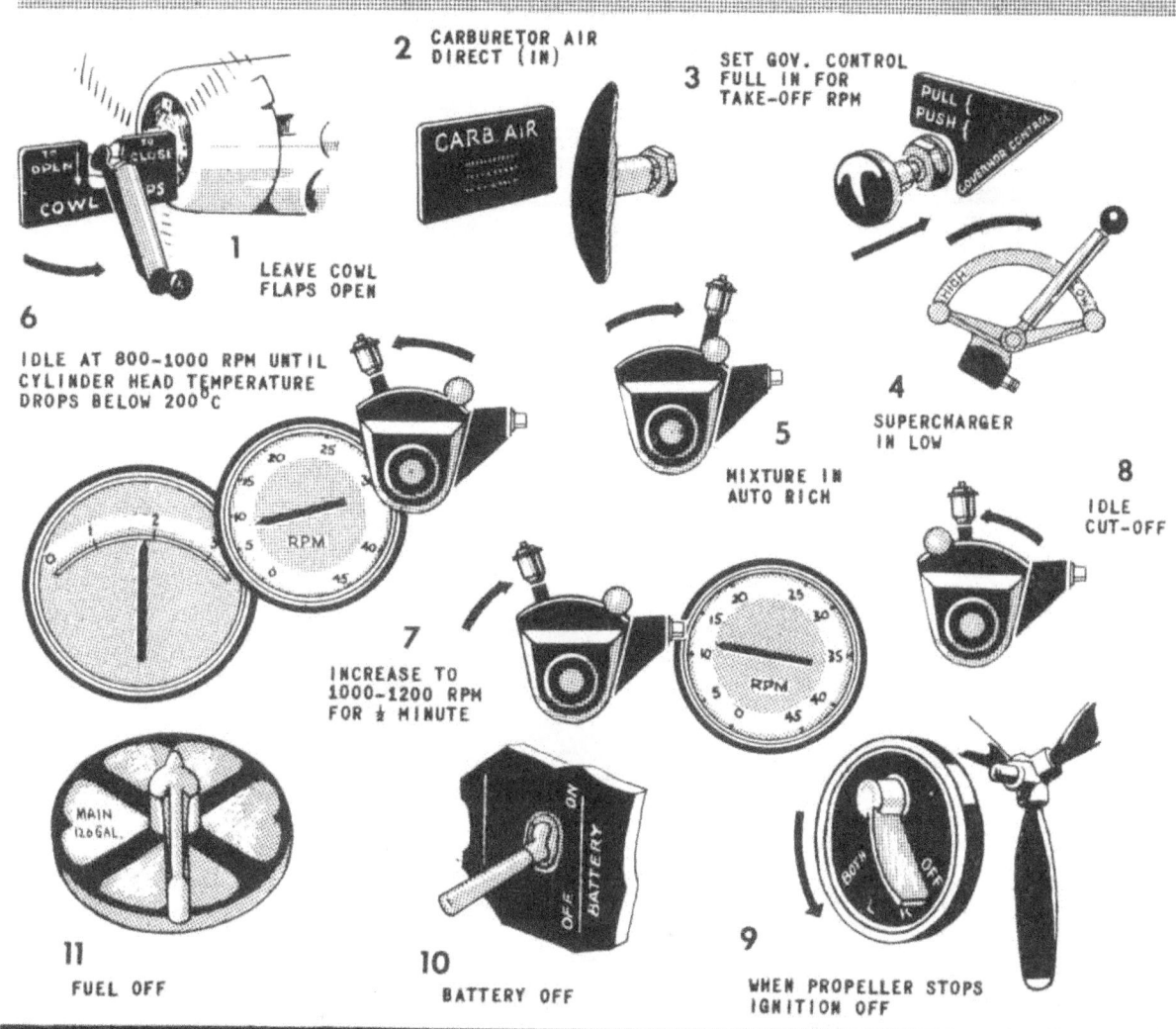

Figure 27—Stopping the Engine

the lubricating oil should be diluted immediately before stopping. Use the following procedure:

(a) Open the shut-off cock in the oil dilution line.

(b) Hold the engine speed constant at 1000 RPM.

(c) Turn the oil dilution switch on and hold it for approximately two minutes.

(d) Still holding the dilution switch on, move the mixture control to *Idle Cut-Off*. Hold the switch on until the engine stops.

(e) Turn off the ignition switch when the propeller stops rotating.

NOTE

When the dilution switch is turned on there will be a sharp drop in indicated fuel pressure.

(2) Precautions:

(a) Do not overdilute.

(b) Guard against fire.

(c) Dilute only when justified by forecast of low temperatures; that is, below −5°C (23°F).

(d) Check the position of the oil dilution shut-off cocks. They should be closed except when actually diluting the oil.

(3) If the oil has been diluted at the last operating period, a normal start and warm-up without rediluting should be made.

21. TIEING DOWN.

a. PARKING HARNESS.—The control parking harness should be carried in the baggage compartment. To

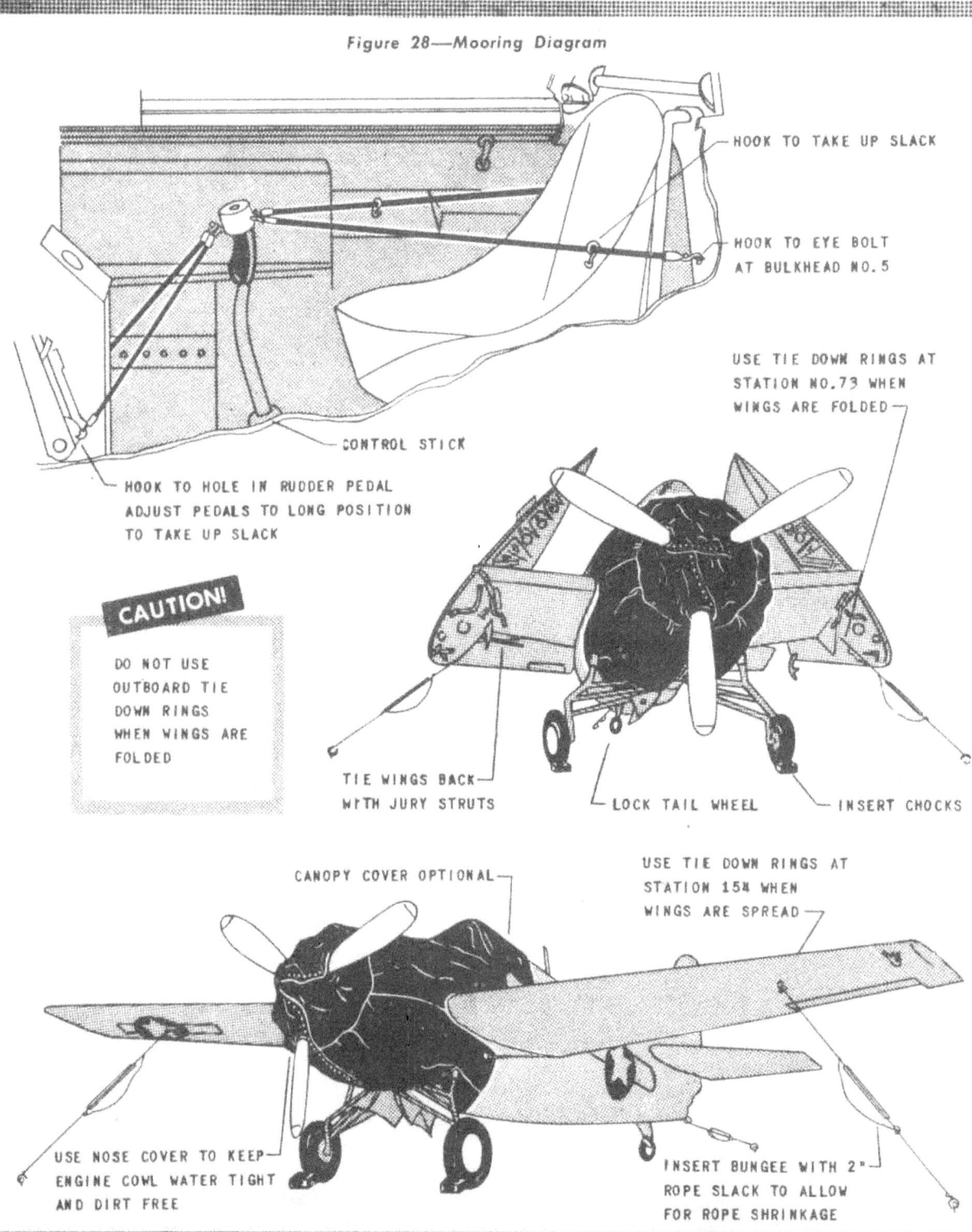

Figure 28—Mooring Diagram

prevent whipping of the control surfaces when the plane must be parked outside, slide the cup of the device over the control stick handle. The two cables fastened to the same ring in the cup are brought forward and hooked into holes in the pedal support arms. The other cables are led aft and hooked into eye-bolts at either side of the pilot's seat and bulkhead No. 5. Slack can be taken up by moving the pedals forward to *Long* position. The spare hooks on the aft cables can be used to take up any additional slack.

b. MOORING.

(1) Lock the tail wheel.

(2) Insert parking blocks.

(3) Slip the nose cover over the engine cowling to keep the engine and accessories dry and dirt-free.

(4) If the wings are folded, use the tie-down rings at Wing Station No. 73. Install the wing covers over the wing fold.

(5) If the wings are spread, use the tie-down rings at Wing Station No. 154.

(6) Attach the tail rope to catapult hold back bolt.

(7) Spread the canvas cabin enclosure cover over the canopy and lash it down.

Section III RESTRICTED
AN 01-190FB-1

POWER PLANT CHART

AIRCRAFT MODEL	PROPELLER	ENGINE MODEL
FM-2	C5325D-A20	R-1820-56W

GAUGE READING	FUEL PRESS.	OIL PRESS.	OIL TEMP. °C	COOLANT TEMP.		OIL(1) CONS.
DESIRED MAXIMUM	17 / 18.5	70 / 75	75-90 / 102			
MINIMUM IDLING	16	65	**60 / 25			

MAXIMUM PERMISSABLE DIVING RPM: 3100 (30 Sec)
MINIMUM RECOMMENDED CRUISE RPM: 1200
MAXIMUM RECOMMENDED TURBO RPM:

OIL GRADE: 1120 SPEC. AN-VV-O-446
FUEL GRADE: 100-130 SPEC. AN-F-28

OPERATING CONDITION	WAR EMERGENCY (COMBAT EMERGENCY)	MILITARY POWER (NON-COMBAT EMERGENCY)		NORMAL RATED (MAXIMUM CONTINUOUS)	MAXIMUM CRUISE (NORMAL OPERATION)
TIME LIMIT	5 MINUTES	30 MINUTES		1 hr. UNLIMITED	UNLIMITED
MAX. CYL. HD. TEMP.	*248°C	232°C		232°C / 218°C	205°C
MIXTURE	*AUTO LEAN	*AUTO LEAN		AUTO LEAN	AUTO LEAN
R.P.M.	2600 (SL-20500) / 2500 (ABOVE 20500)	2600 (SL-20500) / 2500 (ABOVE 20500)		2500	2100

MANIF. PRESS.	SUPER-CHARGER	FUEL(2) Gal/Min	MANIF. PRESS.	SUPER-CHARGER	FUEL(2) Gal/Min	STD. TEMP. °C	PRESSURE ALTITUDE	STD. TEMP. °F	MANIF. PRESS.	SUPER-CHARGER	FUEL GPH(3)	MANIF. PRESS.	SUPER-CHARGER	FUEL GPH(3)
						-55.0	40,000 FT.	-67.0						
						-55.0	38,000 FT.	-67.0						
						-55.0	36,000 FT.	-67.0						
						-52.4	34,000 FT.	-62.3						
						-48.4	32,000 FT.	-55.1						
FULL THROTTLE	HIGH (shift where M.P. drops to 42" in LOW)	.97	THROTTLE AT TAKE-OFF POSITION (46.5" of Sea Level)	HIGH	.97	-44.4	30,000 FT.	-48.0	38" Maximum	HIGH	58	30" Maximum	HIGH	39
		1.20			1.20	-40.5	28,000 FT.	-40.9			72			42
		1.37			1.37	-36.5	26,000 FT.	-33.7			82			45
		1.47			1.47	-32.5	24,000 FT.	-26.5			88			53
		1.67			1.67	-28.6	22,000 FT.	-19.4			100			62
		1.83			1.83	-24.6	20,000 FT.	-12.3			105			64
		2.07			2.07	-20.7	18,000 FT.	-5.2			105			62
		2.15			2.02	-16.7	16,000 FT.	2.0			105			57
		2.30			2.00	-12.7	14,000 FT.	9.1			105			54
		2.42			1.83	-8.8	12,000 FT.	16.2			103			59
		2.50		LOW	1.93	-4.8	10,000 FT.	23.4	43" Maximum	LOW	110	29" Maximum	LOW	61
		2.67			2.07	-0.8	8,000 FT.	30.5			120			56
		2.20			2.20	3.1	6,000 FT.	37.6			128			53
	LOW	2.42			2.42	7.1	4,000 FT.	44.7			128			50
		2.67			2.50	11.0	2,000 FT.	51.8			128			48
		2.75			2.47	15.0	SEA LEVEL	59.0			128			45

GENERAL NOTES

(1) OIL CONSUMPTION: MAXIMUM U.S. QUART PER HOUR PER ENGINE.
(2) Gal/Min: APPROXIMATE U.S. GALLON PER MINUTE PER ENGINE.
(3) GPH: APPROXIMATE U.S. GALLON PER HOUR PER ENGINE.
F.T.: MEANS FULL THROTTLE OPERATION.
VALUES ARE FOR LEVEL FLIGHT WITH RAM.

FOR COMPLETE CRUISING DATA SEE APPENDIX I
NOTE: TO DETERMINE CONSUMPTION IN BRITISH IMPERIAL UNITS, MULTIPLY BY 10 THEN DIVIDE BY 12. RED FIGURES ARE PRELIMINARY SUBJECT TO REVISION AFTER FLIGHT CHECK.

TAKE-OFF CONDITIONS: 2600 RPM—46.5 in.Hg—AUTO RICH—DIRECT AIR (5 MINUTE LIMIT) 248°C MAXIMUM HEAD TEMPERATURE.

CONDITIONS TO AVOID:

SPECIAL NOTES

*OPERATION IN AUTO LEAN IS CONTINGENT ON MAINTAINING HEAD TEMPERATURES BELOW LIMITS.

**30°C (86°F) MINIMUM FOR NORMAL TAKE-OFF. 20°C (68°F) MINIMUM FOR EMERGENCY TAKE-OFF.

SYMBOLS:
✢ — SHIFT BLOWER AT THIS ALTITUDE.

DATA AS OF 12-23-44

Figure 29 —Power Plant Chart
(Sheet 1 of 2 Sheets)

RESTRICTED
AN 01-190FB-1

Section III

POWER PLANT CHART

AIRCRAFT MODEL	PROPELLER	ENGINE MODEL
FM-2	C5325D-A20	R-1820-56

GAUGE READING	FUEL PRESS.	OIL PRESS.	OIL TEMP.	COOLANT TEMP.	OIL[(1)] CONS.		
DESIRED MAXIMUM	17 18.5	70 75	75-90 102			MAXIMUM PERMISSABLE DIVING RPM: 3100 (30 SEC.) MINIMUM RECOMMENDED CRUISE RPM: 1200 MAXIMUM RECOMMENDED TURBO RPM:	
MINIMUM IDLING	16	65 25	**60			OIL GRADE: 1120, SPEC. AN-VV-O-446 FUEL GRADE: 100 130, SPEC. AN-F-28	

WAR EMERGENCY (COMBAT EMERGENCY)			MILITARY POWER (NON-COMBAT EMERGENCY)			OPERATING CONDITION			NORMAL RATED (MAXIMUM CONTINUOUS)			MAXIMUM CRUISE (NORMAL OPERATION)		
MINUTES			30 MINUTES 232°C			TIME LIMIT MAX. CYL. HD. TEMP.			1 HR UNLIMITED 232°C 218°C			UNLIMITED 205°C		
			*AUTO LEAN 2600 (SL-20500) 2500 (ABOVE 20500)			MIXTURE R.P.M.			*AUTO LEAN 2500			AUTO LEAN 2100		
MANIF. PRESS.	SUPER- CHARGER	FUEL[(2)] Gal/Min	MANIF. PRESS.	SUPER- CHARGER	FUEL[(2)] Gal/Min	STD. TEMP. °C	PRESSURE ALTITUDE	STD. TEMP. °F	MANIF. PRESS.	SUPER- CHARGER	FUEL GPH[(1)]	MANIF. PRESS.	SUPER- CHARGER	FUEL GPH[(3)]
						-55.0 -55.0 -55.0	40,000 FT. 38,000 FT. 36,000 FT.	-67.0 -67.0 -67.0						
			F.T.		97	-52.4 -48.4 -44.4	34,000 FT. 32,000 FT. 30,000 FT.	-62.3 -55.1 -48.0	F.T.		58	F.T.		39
			F.T. F.T. F.T.		1.20 1.37 1.47	-40.5 -36.5 -32.5	28,000 FT. 26,000 FT. 24,000 FT.	-40.9 -33.7 -26.5	F.T. F.T. F.T.		72 82 88	F.T. F.T. F.T.		42 45 53
			F.T. F.T. F.T.	HIGH	1.67 1.83 2.07	-28.6 -24.6 -20.7	22,000 FT. 20,000 FT. 18,000 FT.	-19.4 -12.3 -5.2	F.T. 38 38	HIGH	100 105 103	F.T. 30 30	HIGH	62 64 62
			43 43 F.T.		2.02 2.00 1.83	-16.7 -12.7 -8.8	16,000 FT. 14,000 FT. 12,000 FT.	2.0 9.1 16.2	38 38 F.T.		101 100 103	30 30 F.T.		57 54 59
			F.T. F.T. F.T.	LOW	1.93 2.07 2.20	-4.8 -0.8 3.1	10,000 FT. 8,000 FT. 6,000 FT.	23.4 30.5 37.6		LOW	110 120 128	29 29 29	LOW	61 56 53
			F.T. 46.5 46.5		2.42 2.50 2.47	7.1 11.0 15.0	4,000 FT. 2,000 FT. SEA LEVEL	44.7 51.8 58.0	43 43 43		130 128 128	29 29 29		50 48 45

GENERAL NOTES

[(1)] OIL CONSUMPTION: MAXIMUM U.S. QUART PER HOUR PER ENGINE.
[(2)] Gal/Min: APPROXIMATE U.S. GALLON PER MINUTE PER ENGINE.
[(3)] GPH: APPROXIMATE U.S. GALLON PER HOUR PER ENGINE.
F.T.: MEANS FULL THROTTLE OPERATION.
VALUES ARE FOR LEVEL FLIGHT WITH RAM.

FOR COMPLETE CRUISING DATA SEE APPENDIX II
NOTE: TO DETERMINE CONSUMPTION IN BRITISH IMPERIAL UNITS, MULTIPLY BY 10 THEN DIVIDE BY 12. RED FIGURES ARE PRELIMINARY SUBJECT TO REVISION AFTER FLIGHT CHECK.

TAKE-OFF CONDITIONS: 2600 RPM—46.5 in. Hg.
—AUTO RICH—DIRECT AIR—(5 MINUTE LIMIT)
248°C MAX. CYL. HD. TEMP.

CONDITIONS TO AVOID:

SPECIAL NOTES

* OPERATION IN AUTO LEAN IS CONTINGENT ON MAINTAINING HEAD TEMPERATURES BELOW LIMITS.

** 30°C (86°F) MINIMUM FOR NORMAL TAKE-OFF. 20°C (68°F) MINIMUM FOR EMERGENCY TAKE-OFF.

DATA AS OF 12-27-44   BASED ON

Figure 29—Power Plant Chart
(Sheet 2 of 2 Sheets)

RESTRICTED
AN 01-190FB-1

THIS PAGE INTENTIONALLY LEFT BLANK.

Section 3
OPERATING DATA

1. POWER PLANT CHART.

This chart is intended to summarize the specific characteristics and limitations of the engine and to provide additional instructions and information. The Engine Calibration Curve should be used to supplement the data given here. The definitions of the engine power ratings as shown on the chart are as follows:

a. TAKE-OFF.—Maximum recommended for take-off under a five minute time limit.

b. WAR EMERGENCY.—The limits established by the manufacturer and accepted by the Government specifically for combat use under the specified time limit, limited to five minutes duration.

c. MILITARY.—Maximum recommended for operation limited to thirty minutes duration.

d. NORMAL RATED (Maximum Continuous).—Maximum recommended for continuous operation.

e. MAXIMUM CRUISE.—Maximum continuous cruising recommended for operation with lean mixture under a specified cylinder head temperature limit.

2. AIR SPEED CORRECTION TABLE.

Figure 27 is an Airspeed Indicator Calibration Chart showing the relationship between indicated and actual airspeed in knots.

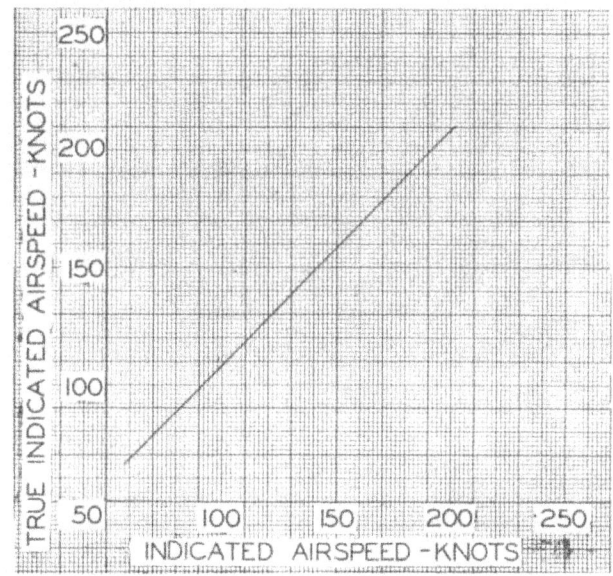

Figure 30—

Air Speed Correction Table

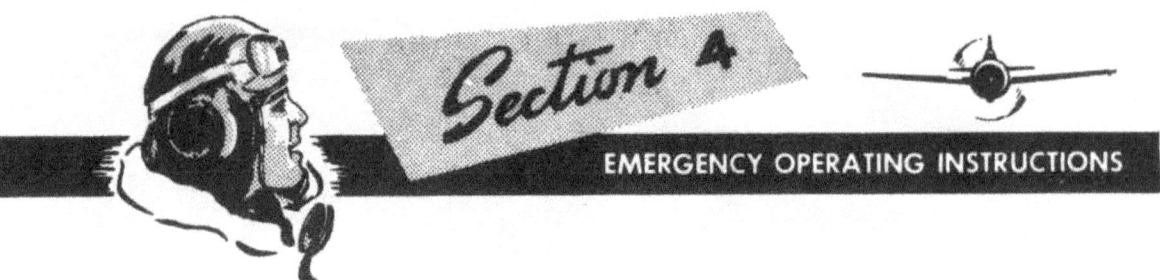

EMERGENCY OPERATING INSTRUCTIONS

1. SLIDING CANOPY EMERGENCY RELEASE.

To jettison the sliding canopy for emergency exit, grasp the red painted rings on both sides at the forward end of the canopy and pull aft. This removes the pins holding the canopy to the track slide allowing the slip-stream to tear the canopy free. It may be necessary to give the canopy a slight push up into the air stream if it is in a full closed position when the rings are pulled.

CAUTION

The pilot must pull the two emergency release pins simultaneously so that both sides of the canopy will be freed at approximately the same time. Should one pin be pulled before the other the pilot may be trapped or injured if the airstream jams the canopy on the remaining pin or whips it over as it is being torn free.

2. FIRES.

Open the canopy and gain as much altitude as possible.

a. ENGINE FIRES.—Although no absolute rule can be made to control a fire in the engine section, the following procedure is offered as a guiding principle to be followed in the order listed in case of fire in flight or on the ground.

(1) Turn the fuel selector valve to the *Off* position, thus stopping the flow of fuel to the fire. Do not cut the engine switch.

(2) Close the cowl flaps.

(3) Push the carburetor air control in for direct air supply.

(4) Increase the engine power as much as circumstances permit in order to consume the fuel that might otherwise feed the fire.

b. WING FIRES.

(1) If a fire is discovered in either wing turn off the following switches and rheostats controlling electrical units and wiring in the wing:

 Gun Camera Switch
 Gun Master Switch
 Formation Light Switch
 Wing Running Light Switch
 Pilot Tube Heater Switch

Figure 31—Cockpit Emergency Exit

(2) Attempt to extinguish the fire by sideslipping.

3. ENGINE FAILURE.

In case of engine failure with altitude, put the mixture control into *Auto Rich,* retard the throttle to a maximum of 20 in. Hg, throw on the emergency fuel pump switch, and hold the primer switch in *On.* Do not try to exceed 20 in. Hg manifold pressure while operating on the primer. Open the canopy.

Glide for flying speed. Further glide can be obtained with the flaps up. If the engine does not catch for a power landing and the location makes it possible to bring the airplane in, cut the ignition and turn the fuel selector valve to *Off* before landing. Lower the flaps when approaching for the landing.

4. WHEELS UP LANDING.

If the landing gear should fail to come down, land as slowly as possible with flaps down. Open the canopy. Level the airplane off about ten feet or less above the ground and let it drop in.

5. WATER LANDING—DITCHING.

If it becomes necessary to make a water landing, head for deep water. A landing in shallow water might cause the airplane to overturn and trap the pilot if the nose hits the bottom upon settling. Lock the canopy "OPEN". Keep the landing gear up and come in as for a wheels-up landing. As the airplane hits the water and loses forward momentum the nose will settle deeper and deeper and finally sink nose first. However, before the airplane makes its final plunge the pilot will have time to escape.

6. GENERATOR FAILURE.

If generator failure occurs in flight:

a. Turn off all electrically operated devices not essential to safety in order to conserve the battery.

b. With the Propeller Selector Switch on *Fixed Pitch* change the propeller pitch to the best fixed pitch for normal flight. Do not use the Automatic Setting.

c. Conserve the battery by:

(1) Using the radio sparingly.

(2) Turn off the battery switch as much as safe operation will permit. Turn it on only periodically as required to read the instruments and perform other necessary operations.

d. Turn on the battery switch before landing in order to have all electrical devices functioning normally during the landing. Set the propeller selector switch in *Automatic* position.

7. MP REGULATOR FAILURE.

Should the MP Regulator fail, approximately 90% of Normal Rated Power is available through the mechanical linkage between the throttle control lever and the carburetor throttle. The 10% lost represents that portion of the carburetor movement controlled by the automatic action of the Regulator.

In case of such failure operate the throttle control lever as though the Regulator was not installed in the linkage, advancing it to maintain the desired MP during a climb and retarding it during descent.

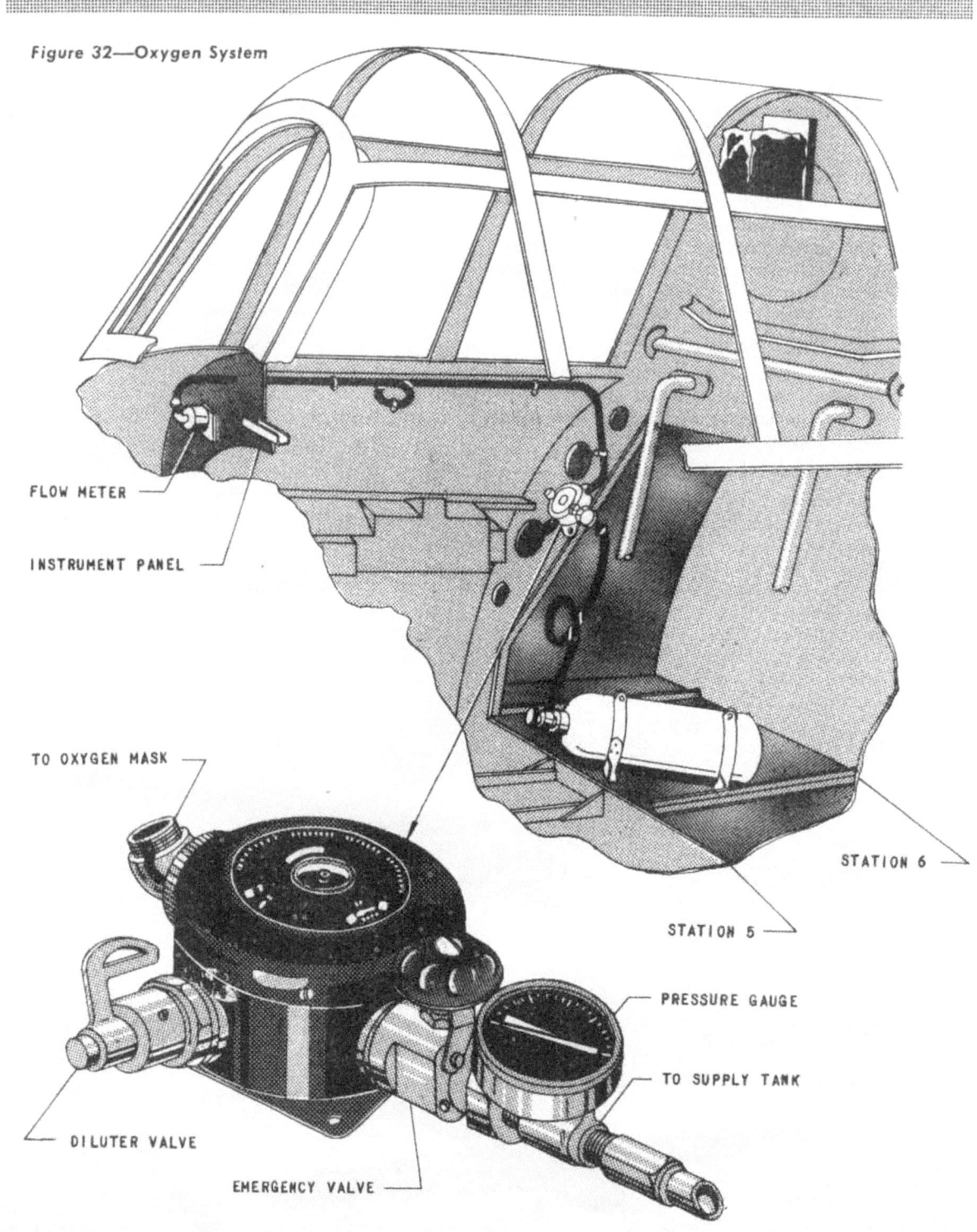

Figure 32—Oxygen System

Section 5
OPERATIONAL EQUIPMENT

1. OXYGEN SYSTEM.

a. DESCRIPTION.—This airplane has provisions for the installation of the diluter-demand oxygen system. The regulator is mounted on the bulkhead to the right and aft of the pilot. The pressure gage is mounted at the intake port of the regulator. The flowmeter is mounted in the right hand instrument panel facing the pilot. The tank itself is mounted in a cradle behind the pilot's seat. The main control handwheel is on the forward end of the oxygen cylinder to the right of the pilot's seat.

CAUTION

Oxygen equipment must be kept free from oil, grease and easily oxydized materials.

b. OPERATION.

(1) GENERAL.—The diluter-demand regulator opens a valve to provide a flow of oxygen during each inhalation. The emergency by-pass valve, incorporated in the regulator unit, provides a continuous flow of oxygen directly from the cylinder. The diluter valve allows air from the cockpit to enter the breathing system. The amount of air admitted by this valve is dependent upon the altitude up to approximately 30,000 feet beyond which 100 per cent oxygen is delivered.

During normal operations the diluter lever should be turned to the *On* position thus obtaining the maximum economy and endurance from the oxygen supply aboard the plane. However, if the presence of carbon monoxide in the cockpit is suspected as the result of the break-down of normal sealing of the fuselage or of damage by gunfire, the diluter lever should be turned to *Off* position. In this position 100% oxygen is supplied, but only during each inhalation. 100% oxygen is also supplied with the Emergency By-Pass valve *On*, but in a continuous flow regardless of the cycle of breathing.

All personnel using oxygen equipment should familiarize themselves thoroughly with the symptoms of anoxia as described in Technical Note 30-41 so that they will at all times be on the alert to detect oxygen deficiencies before serious physical defects have been encountered.

(2) WHEN TO USE OXYGEN.—The pilot should use the oxygen equipment with the diluter valve set to the *On* position, except as noted above:

(*a*) On all flights when above 10,000 feet.

(*b*) On flights of more than four hours duration between 8 to 10,000 feet for a minimum of fifteen minutes out of every hour.

(*c*) On *night* flights when above 5,000 feet.

c. PRE-FLIGHT CHECK.—To assure proper functioning of the oxygen system, the following items should be checked while the plane is on the ground prior to a flight in which oxygen is to be used or is likely to be used.

(1) Close the Emergency Valve.

(2) Open the cylinder valve. Allow at least ten seconds for the pressure in line to equalize. The pressure gage should then read 1800 ± 50 p.s.i. if the cylinder is fully charged.

(3) Close the cylinder valve. If the pressure drops more than 100 pounds in five minutes there is excessive leakage. In such a case the oxygen system should be repaired prior to use.

(4) Check the mask fit by placing the thumb over the end of the mask tube and inhale lightly. If there is no leakage, the mask will adhere tightly to the face due to the suction created. If the mask leaks, tighten the mask suspension straps and/or adjust the nose wire and repeat the above test. *Do Not Use a Mask That Leaks.*

CAUTION

Never check mask fit by squeezing the mask tube *while the Emergency Valve is On.*

(5) Couple the mask securely to the breathing tube by means of the quick disconnect coupling.

CAUTION

Mating parts of coupling must not be "cocked" but be fully engaged.

(6) Open the cylinder valve. Depress the diaphragm knob through the hole in the center of the regulator case and feel the flow of oxygen into the mask. Then release the diaphragm knob. Breathe several times observing the oxygen flow indicator for "blink", verifying the positive flow of oxygen.

> **NOTE**
>
> Since the amount of oxygen added is very small at sea level the oxygen flow meter may not operate while the airplane is on the ground. In this case turn the air-valve to *Off* or *100% Oxygen* and test again. If the oxygen flow indicator operation is now satisfactory, reset the air-valve to *On* or *Normal Oxygen*. In this setting adequate oxygen flow and "blinker" operation will be assured at oxygen altitudes.

(7) Check the Emergency Valve by slowly turning it counter-clockwise until the oxygen flows vigorously into the mask, then close the Emergency Valve.

> **NOTE**
>
> Upon completion of an oxygen check or an oxygen flight, close the cylinder valve.

d. RECHARGING CYLINDER.—To allow a safe margin of oxygen for maximum usage during a single flight, be sure that tank pressure is at 1800 PSI before any takeoff for an oxygen flight. At no time should the residual pressure in the tank be allowed to fall below 300 PSI.

The cylinder must be removed from the airplane to be recharged. Close the cylinder valve tightly, disconnect the tube at the valve and remove the cylinder from the cradle. *Be sure to close the valve before disconnecting the cylinder line.* High pressure oxygen escaping from a cylinder transforms it into a battering ram.

The cylinder is then connected to the recharge equipment by means of the sleeve nut on the valve. The cylinder valve is opened allowing the oxygen to cascade into the cylinder as the recharge equipment is operated until a pressure of 1900-1950 PSI is indicated. This pressure is necessary to insure 1800 PSI after the oxygen temperature in the cylinder has dropped from that caused by flow. Shut off the valve tightly and reinstall the cylinder in the airplane. The exact method of charging the cylinder will vary with the recharging equipment used.

> **CAUTION**
>
> Exercise the greatest care to prevent oil, grease, white lead or any other easily oxidized material from coming in contact with the oxygen equipment. Contact of such materials with oxygen under pressure may cause explosion.

e. MAN-HOUR OXYGEN CONSUMPTION TABLE.—Figure 33 consists of a man-hour oxygen consumption table showing the endurance obtainable with the air-valve in the *On* and *Off* positions until the pressure falls to 300 PSI.

For example, if a flight of 5 hours duration at 18,500 feet is planned, reference to this table shows that sufficient oxygen is available for the flight only with the air valve set to the *On* position. If, however, a flight with droppable fuel tanks of 9.8 hours duration is planned at 18,500 feet, reference to this table shows that a flight of such a duration can only be made at 15,000 feet altitude.

In preparing his flight plan, the pilot should always check his proposed time of flight in altitudes above 10,000 feet against the accompanying chart to be certain sufficient oxygen is available for the flight.

2. OPERATION OF RADIO EQUIPMENT.

a. DESCRIPTION.

(1) GENERAL.—The FM-2 airplanes are equipped with three different radio installations. All the installations will eventually be changed in service to accommodate the AN/ARC-1 Communication Equipment, the AN/ARR-2 Navigation Equipment, and the BC1206 Range Receiver provided for ferry and training operations. This installation will be identical to the installation being incorporated in production on airplanes serial No. 57044 and subsequent with the exception of a slight difference in Navigation Equipment. The AN/ARR-2 Navigation Equipment incorporates a mechanical means

ENDURANCE WITH 514 CUBIC INCH CYLINDER

Altitude	Diluter Demand Regulator—Set to *Off* or *100% Oxygen*	Diluter Demand Regulator—Set to *On* or *Normal Oxygen*
5,000 feet	1.8 hours	7.0 hours
10,000 feet	2.1 hours	8.3 hours
15,000 feet	2.6 hours	10.0 hours
20,000 feet	3.3 hours	8.8 hours
25,000 feet	4.1 hours	6.0 hours
30,000 feet	5.0 hours	5.0 hours
35,000 feet	6.5 hours	6.5 hours

Figure 33—

Man-Hour Oxygen

Consumption Table

of selecting the desired operating channels, while the AN/ARR-2a incorporates an automatic electrical selection of the channels.

In all installations, the radio controls are located on the starboard side of the cockpit aft of the Pilot's Distribution panel. A switch for a throat microphone is built in the throttle control. All other equipment is located in the baggage compartment.

NOTE

When the engine is running the battery switch need not be *On* to operate the radio equipment as the operating current is drawn from the generator and/or the battery when the engine is running. The battery switch *should* be turned *On*, however to care for the peak loads.

(2) Airplanes serial number 15952 to serial number 46942 inclusive are supplied with GF-12/RU-17 Communication Equipment, ZB-3(AN/ARR-1) Navigation Equipment, provision for ABD/ABE Navigation Equipment, provision for ABA-1 Identification Equipment, and provision for IFF/ABK Identification Equipment. Refer to figure 34 for a photograph of this equipment.

(3) Airplanes serial number 46943 to 57043 inclusive are supplied with AN/ARC-4 Communication Equipment, AN/ARR-2 Navigation Equipment, BC1206 Range Receiver, AN/APX-1 IFF Equipment and provision for ABA-1 Identification Equipment. Refer to figure 35 for a photograph of this equipment.

(4) Airplanes serial number 57044 and subsequent are supplied with AN/ARC-1 Communication Equipment, AN/ARR-2a Navigation Equipment, BC1206 Range Equipment, AN/APX-1 IFF Equipment and provision for ABA-1 Identification Equipment. Refer to figure 36 for a photograph of this equipment.

CAUTION

Operation of this equipment involves use of high voltages which are dangerous and may result in fatal injuries. Operating personnel must, therefore, observe all safety regulations at all times.

b. OPERATION OF COMMUNICATION EQUIPMENT.

(1) GF-12/RU-17 COMMUNICATION EQUIPMENT.

(*a*) TO RECEIVE.

1. Set the Navigation Communication switch on *Communication*.

2. Set the ICS-Radio Switch on *Radio*.

3. Set the Auto-Off-Manual switch on *Auto* or *Manual*.

4. Turn the dual coil set remote control to the desired frequency band.

5. Tune and receive by means of the remote tuner.

6. If operating in *Manual*, adjust the volume with the *Increase-Output* knob.

7. If receiving voice or a modulated signal, use the *MCW* switch position.

8. If receiving an unmodulated signal, use the *CW* switch position.

(*b*) TO TRANSMIT VOICE.

1. Set the *ICS-Radio* switch on *Radio*.

2. Set the *Auto-Off-Manual* switch on *Manual* or *Auto*.

3. Set the *Voice-CW - MCW* switch on *Voice*.

4. Press the *Press to Talk* switch on the microphone or the switch in the throttle control arm if an oxygen mask is being worn.

(*c*) TO TRANSMIT IN CODE.

1. Set the *ICS-Radio* switch on *Radio*.

2. Set the *Auto-Off-Manual* switch on *Manual* or *Auto*.

3. Set the *Voice-CW - MCW* switch on *CW* or *MCW*.

4. Press the code key on the transmitter control box.

(2) AN/ARC-4 COMMUNICATION EQUIPMENT.

(*a*) TO RECEIVE.

1. Turn off the Output Control on the Navigation Receiver Control unit (full counter clockwise).

2. Set the Communication Control Unit *On-Off* switch to *On*.

3. Set the *Radio-Interphone* switch on *Radio*. (This position will always be maintained with this installation).

4. Set the *P-G, Both, P-P* switch for *P-P* (Plane to plane).

5. Advance the volume control (Increase-Output control knob) clockwise for desired reception. Channel 1 will now be received regardless of the position of the Channel Selector switch.

6. The following table lists receiving and transmitting channels for each position of the Channel Selector switch and the *P-G, Both, P-P* switch:

Channel Selection Position	Transmitter Channel	Receiver Channels for each Position of P-G, Both, P-P switch		
		P-P	Both	P-G
1	1	1	1 & 2	2
2	2	1	1 & 2	2
3	3	1	1 & 3	3
4	4	1	1 & 4	4

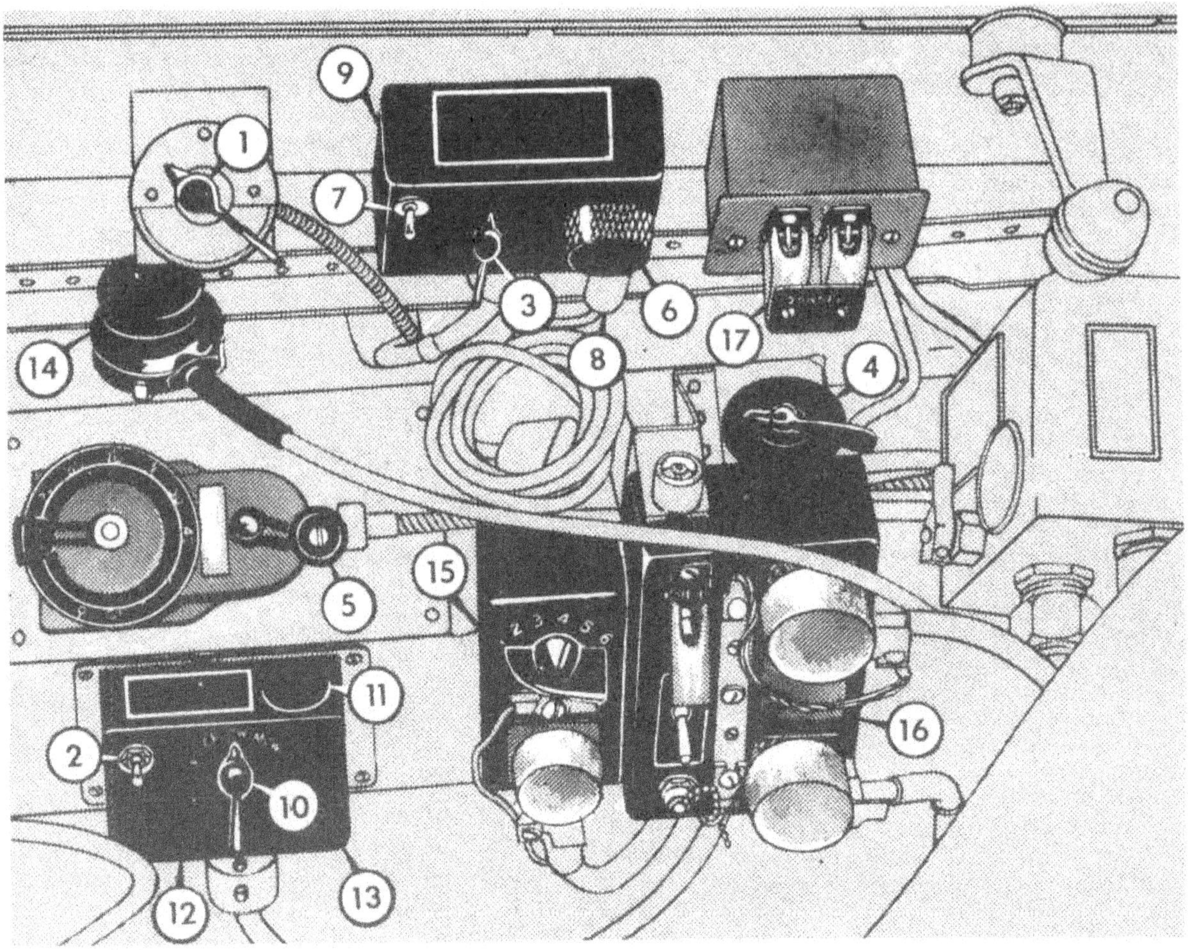

Section V

RESTRICTED
AN 01-190FB-1

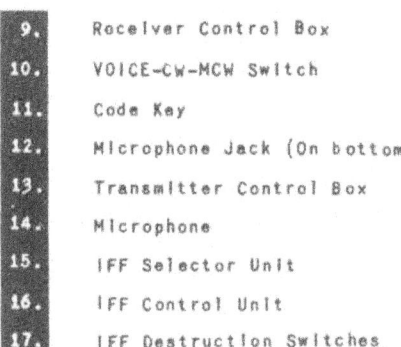

1. NAVIGATION-COMMUNICATION Switch
2. ICS-RADIO Switch
3. AUTO-OFF-MANUAL Switch
4. Dual Coil Remote Control
5. Remote Tuner
6. Volume INCREASE-OUTPUT Knob
7. CW-MCW Switch
8. Headphone Jack (On bottom)
9. Receiver Control Box
10. VOICE-CW-MCW Switch
11. Code Key
12. Microphone Jack (On bottom)
13. Transmitter Control Box
14. Microphone
15. IFF Selector Unit
16. IFF Control Unit
17. IFF Destruction Switches

Figure 34—GF-12/RU-17 and ZB-3 Radio Equipment

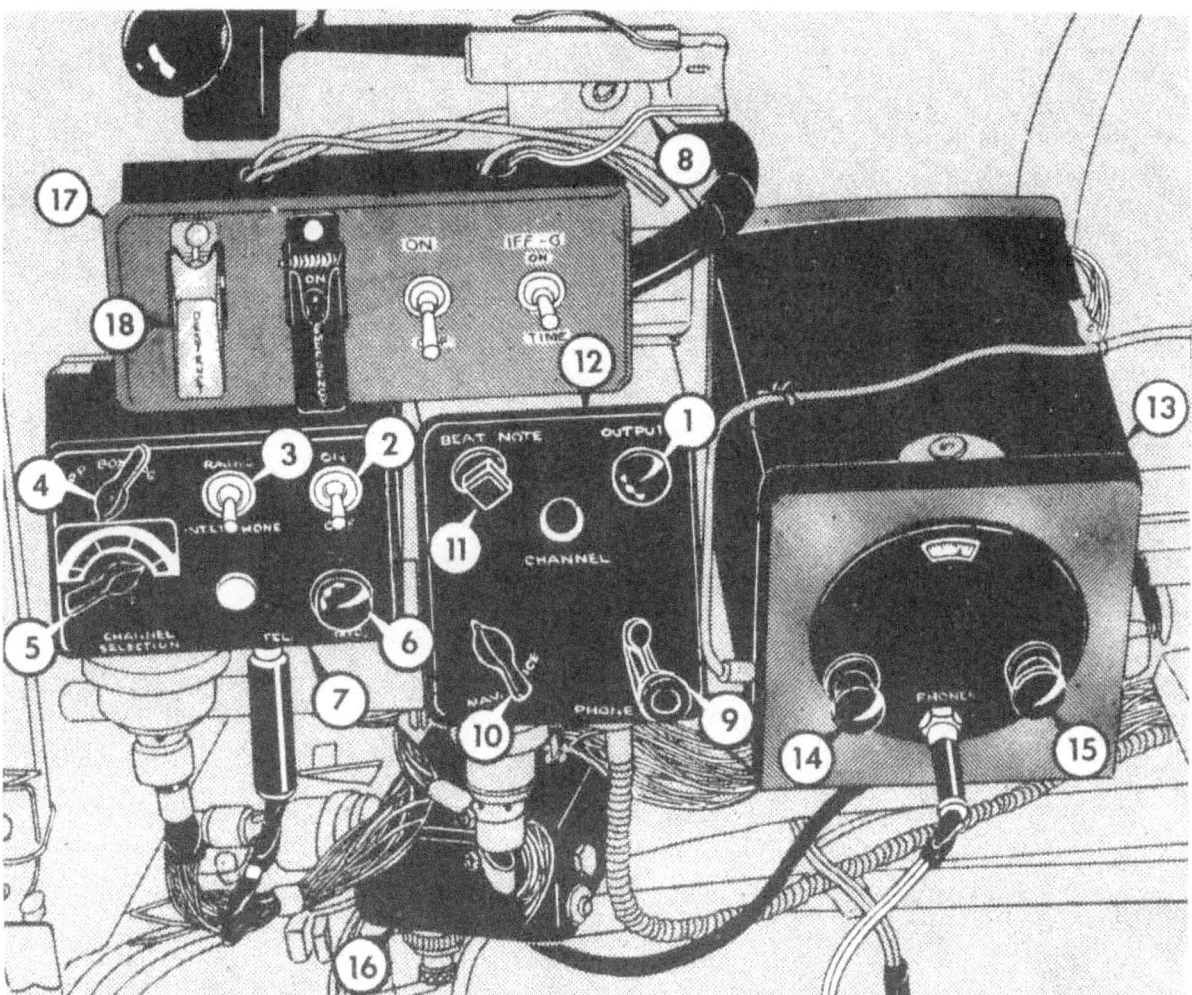

1. Volume INCREASE-OUTPUT Knob (Navigation)
2. ON-OFF Switch
3. RADIO-INTERPHONE Switch
4. PG-BOTH-PP Swithh
5. CHANNEL SELECTION Switch
6. Volume INCREASE-OUTPUT Knob (Communication)
7. Communication Control Unit
8. Microphone Bracket
9. Channel Crank Handle
10. NAVIGATION-VOICE Selector Switch
11. BEAT NOTE Knob
12. Navigation Control Unit
13. BC 1206 Range Receiver
14. ON-OFF Volume Control Switch
15. Tuner
16. Jack Box
17. IFF Control Box
18. IFF Destruction Switch

Figure 35—AN/ARC-4 and AN/ARR-2 Radio Equipment

Section V
RESTRICTED
AN 01-190FB-1

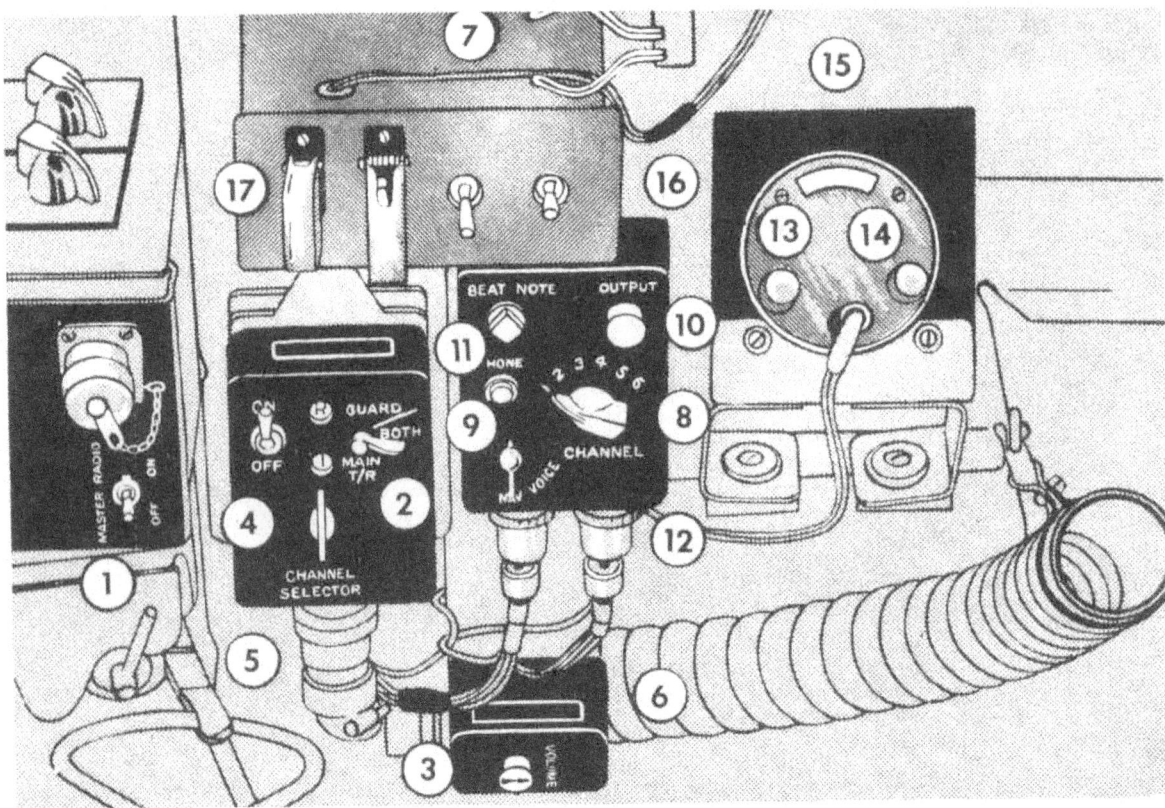

1.	MASTER RADIO Switch	9.	NAVIGATION-VOICE Switch
2.	GUARD-BOTH-MAIN Switch	10.	Volume INCREASE OUTPUT Control
3.	Volume Control	11.	BEAT NOTE Knob
4.	Channel Selector Switch	12.	Navigation Control Unit
5.	Communications Control Unit	13.	On-Off Volume Control
6.	Jack Box	14.	Tuner Knob
7.	Microphone Bracket	15.	BC-1206 Range Receiver
8.	Channel Selector Switch	16.	IFF Control Box
		17.	IFF Destruction Switch

Figure 36—AN/ARC-1 and AN/ARR-2a Radio Equipment

(b) TO TRANSMIT.

1. Obtain the desired operating channel in accordance with the above table. The transmitting channel is indicated directly by the channel indicator.

2. Press the *Press to Talk* switch on the microphone or the switch in the throttle control arm if an oxygen mask is being worn.

NOTE

Voice transmission only is possible with this equipment.

(3) AN/ARC-1 COMMUNICATION EQUIPMENT.

(a) TO RECEIVE.

1. Set the Radio Master Switch on the side of the Pilot's Distribution panel to *On*.

2. Select *Guard, Both* or *Main* channels.

3. Obtain desired volume by turning the volume control knob on the jack box clockwise.

4. The following table lists reception and transmitting channels for each position of the Channel Selector switch:

Channel Selection Position	Channels Available	
	Transmitting	Receiving
Guard	Guard	Guard
Both	1-9, incl.	Guard & 1-9, incl.
Main T/R	1-9, incl.	1-9, incl.

(b) TO TRANSMIT.

1. Set the Radio Master Switch to *On*.

2. Set the Channel Selector switch to the channel in which transmission is desired in accordance with the above table.

3. Press the *Press to Talk* switch on the microphone, or the switch in the throttle control arm if an oxygen mask is being worn.

NOTE

Voice transmission only is provided on this equipment.

c. OPERATION OF NAVIGATION EQUIPMENT.

(1) ZB-3 NAVIGATION EQUIPMENT.

(a) With Communication Equipment set for receiving as previously described under 2 *b* (1) *(a)*, set the Communication-Navigation switch or selector on *Navigation*.

(b) Set the *CW-MCW* switch on the receiver switch box on *CW*.

(c) Set the *Auto-Off-Manual* switch on the Receiver switch box on *Manual*.

(d) Set the dual coil set remote control to the desired frequency band.

(e) Turn the Receiver Output control clockwise to *Increase-Output* and adjust the volume as desired.

(2) AN/ARR-2 NAVIGATION EQUIPMENT.

(a) Turn the Output Control knob on the VHF Communication Control unit off (full counter clockwise).

(b) Operate the crank with the Navigation Receiver Control unit to obtain the desired operating channel indicated in the Channel Window.

(c) Set the *Nav-Voice* Selector switch on *Nav*.

(d) Set the Output control to obtain a usable weak signal (turn clockwise). If the desired signal cannot be heard, adjust to obtain a fairly strong background hiss.

(e) Adjust the Beat Note knob to produce a pleasing audible tone.

(f) Readjust the Output control to the minimum required for reception of signals to avoid inaccurate course indications.

(3) AN/ARR-2a NAVIGATION EQUIPMENT. —Operation of this equipment is the same as with the AN/ARR-2 equipment described above with the following exceptions:

(a) In lieu of the first step (step *(a)*, Paragraph (2) above), turn down the volume control of the jack box. This volume control affects the AN/ARC-1 Communication Equipment only.

NOTE

The jack boxes, type J-22A/ARC-5, used with this installation have been modified to provide a direct circuit from the Navigation Equipment to the plug-in receptacle so that the volume control on the jack box regulates the volume of the AN/ARC-1 Communication Equipment only. Due to an electrical phenomenon, reception of the Navigation Equipment is also affected by the jack box volume control. Therefore, it may be necessary to turn the volume control up (clockwise) when using the Navigation Equipment.

(b) The desired channel is obtained by use of a channel selector switch in lieu of the crank.

(4) BC1206 RANGE RECEIVER.

(a) If used in conjunction with the installations referred to in paragraph 2 *a* (3), turn off VHF Communication Receiver by turning the *Increase-Output* control counter-clockwise.

(b) Turn up the volume control. This acts as an On-Off switch in a minimum position.

(c) Tune in the desired station and adjust the volume control. This control should be set to the minimum required for reception to avoid inaccurate course indications.

(d) When step *(a)* is required restore the Output control on the VHF Communication Receiver to a

previous setting if simultaneous monitoring is desired.

> **NOTE**
>
> The secret of accurately interpreting Navigation signals is attained by the lowest practical setting of the Output Control. Keep this control adjusted to receive only one character predominately. The lower the signal level, the better the reception.

d. SIMULTANEOUS RECEPTION OF NAVIGATION AND COMMUNICATION EQUIPMENT.

(1) GF-12/RU17 COMMUNICATION EQUIPMENT AND ZB-3 NAVIGATION EQUIPMENT.—With this installation simultaneous reception is not possible.

(2) AN/ARC-4 COMMUNICATION EQUIPMENT AND AN/ARR-2 NAVIGATION EQUIPMENT.

(a) Set the *On-Off* switch on Communication control unit to *On*.

(b) Turn the *Increase-Output* control clockwise to attain desired reception.

(c) Set the *P-G, Both, P-P* switch on Communication Control unit to *Both*.

(3) AN/ARC-1 COMMUNICATION EQUIPMENT AND AN/ARR-2a NAVIGATION EQUIPMENT.—This installation provides simultaneous reception at all times when Navigation Equipment is in operation.

e. PRE-FLIGHT RADIO TEST.

(1) On entering the cockpit, plug the head-set into the disconnect jack on the phone extension cord.

(2) Check to see that the microphone and head-set plugs are fully engaged in the jack box. If the use of an oxygen mask is anticipated, connect the mask microphone plug to the throttle microphone receptacle.

(3) Turn the battery switch to *On*.

(4) Test the VHF Communication Receiver by checking operation in all channels to be used.

> **WARNING**
>
> This test is subject to local limitations regarding Radio silence.

(5) Test the Navigation Equipment or Range Receiver, depending upon the mission assigned.

(6) When installations permit, set controls for simultaneous reception of Communication and Navigation Equipment.

(7) Select the desired transmitting channel and, if security instructions permit, make a test transmission with the base station and any other plane scheduled to same flight or mission.

Section 6 — EXTREME WEATHER OPERATION

1. GENERAL DISCUSSION.

When operating in any locality where any extreme hot or cold weather conditions exist, or in desert or dry regions where there is an excessive amount of dust and sand in the air, certain precautions or additional operations are necessary to maintain normal and safe operation of this airplane. In extreme cold weather, precautions must be taken to prevent the formation of ice on certain parts of the airplane rendering flight impossible, just as in extreme hot weather steps must be taken to prevent overheating of the engine. The steps necessary for the operation of this airplane under these conditions are set forth in this section.

2. ARCTIC AND COLD WEATHER OPERATION.

a. WINDSHIELD DEFROSTER.—To defrost the windshield of this airplane, pull out the T handle control located above the left rudder pedal just forward of and below the instrument panel. This introduces heated air into the space between the double windshield thus removing and preventing any formation of frost on the windshield.

b. OIL DILUTION.

(1) If temperatures below —5°C (23°F) are forecast for the period just prior to the next expected operation, the lubricating oil should be diluted immediately before stopping the engine. (See Section II, Par. 20*b*.)

c. PITOT TUBE HEATER.—The pitot tube is furnished with an electric heater which is controlled by a switch on the pilot's distribution panel. When icing conditions are encountered the pitot tube switch should be turned *On* to prevent ice formation on or inside the pitot tube resulting in erroneous airspeed indications.

d. ELECTRIC GUN HEATERS.—When operation of the guns is anticipated under icing conditions, the pilot should make sure that the gun heater is plugged in at the inboard gun compartment in each wing before taking off. When plugged in the gun heaters are connected directly to the generator and are *On* whenever the engine is running. Therefore, the pilot has no control of the gun heaters from the cockpit.

3. DESERT AND EXTREME DRY AND DUSTY CLIMATE OPERATION.

When operating under extremely dry and dusty conditions, the pilot should set the carburetor alternate air control for alternate air during landing, take-off, all ground operations and during flight at altitudes where there is an abnormal amount of dust and sand in the air. The alternate air duct of this airplane is provided with a filter that will remove all dust particles before entering the carburetor and engine where sand and dust would cause damage. The loss of ram which will accompany the shift from direct to alternate air supply will result in a drop in manifold pressure, but can always be compensated for by an increased throttle opening except when full throttle is already being used.

4. TROPIC AND EXTREME HOT WEATHER OPERATION.

When operating under extreme hot weather conditions the engine will have a greater tendency to overheat especially during all ground and low altitude operation. The pilot, therefore, must pay more attention to the engine cylinder head temperature and compensate for any overheating with the mixture and cowl flap control.

APPENDIX I

Operating Charts, Tables, Curves and Diagrams

Appendix I of this publication shall not be carried in aircraft on combat missions or when there is a reasonable chance of it falling into the hands of the enemy.

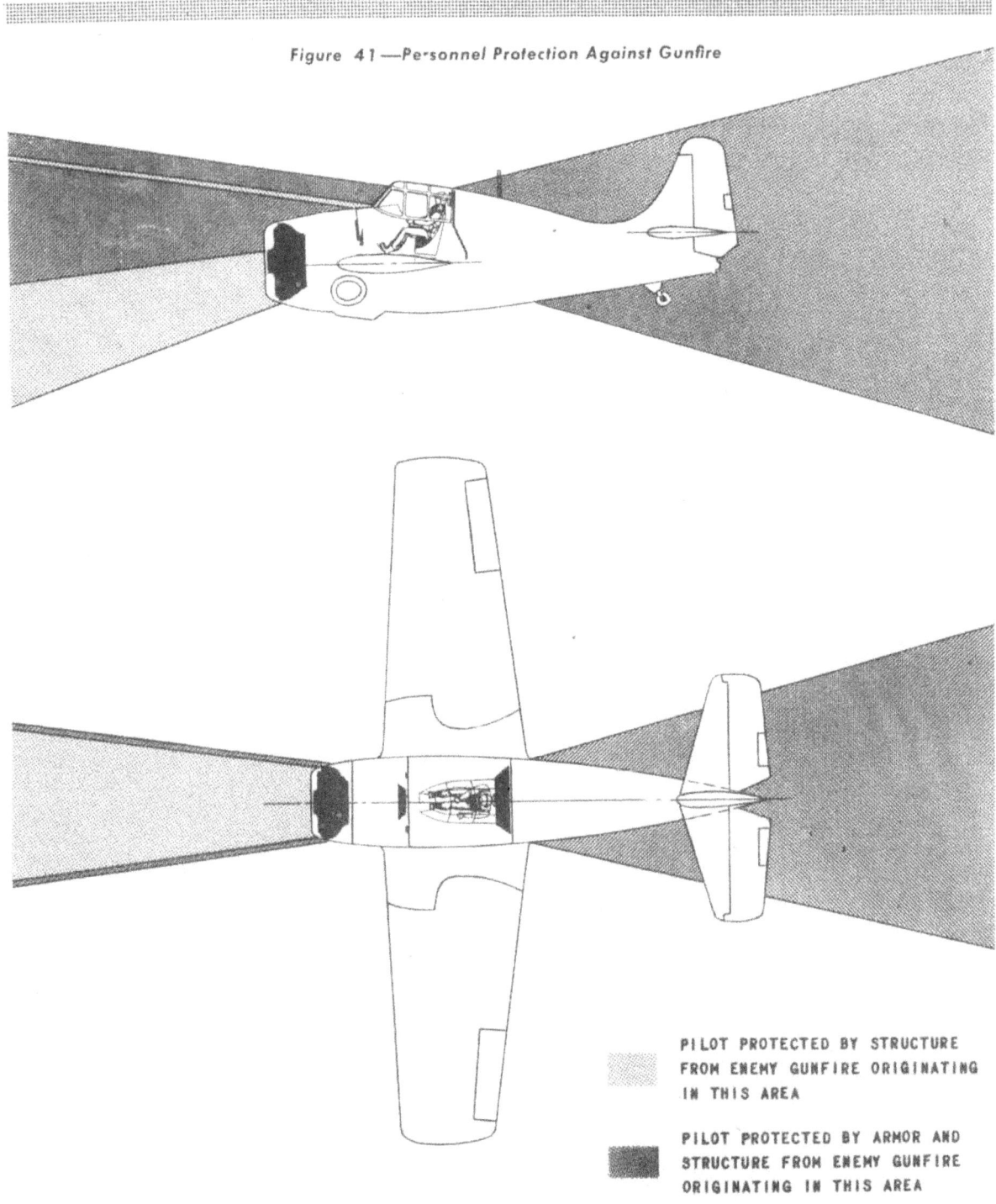

Figure 41—Personnel Protection Against Gunfire

PILOT PROTECTED BY STRUCTURE FROM ENEMY GUNFIRE ORIGINATING IN THIS AREA

PILOT PROTECTED BY ARMOR AND STRUCTURE FROM ENEMY GUNFIRE ORIGINATING IN THIS AREA

Appendix I of this publication shall not be carried in aircraft on combat missions or when there is reasonable chance of its falling into the hands of the enemy.

RESTRICTED
AN 01-190FB-1

Appendix I

TAKE-OFF, CLIMB & LANDING CHART

AIRCRAFT MODEL: FM-2
ENGINE MODEL: R-1820-56

TAKE-OFF DISTANCE - FEET

GROSS WEIGHT LB.	HEAD WIND		HARD SURFACE RUNWAY						SOD-TURF RUNWAY						SOFT SURFACE RUNWAY					
			AT SEA LEVEL		AT 3000 FEET		AT 6000 FEET		AT SEA LEVEL		AT 3000 FEET		AT 6000 FEET		AT SEA LEVEL		AT 3000 FEET		AT 6000 FEET	
	M.P.H.	KTS	GROUND RUN	TO CLEAR 50' OBJ.	GROUND RUN	TO CLEAR 50' OBJ.	GROUND RUN	TO CLEAR 50' OBJ.	GROUND RUN	TO CLEAR 50' OBJ.	GROUND RUN	TO CLEAR 50' OBJ.	GROUND RUN	TO CLEAR 50' OBJ.	GROUND RUN	TO CLEAR 50' OBJ.	GROUND RUN	TO CLEAR 50' OBJ.	GROUND RUN	TO CLEAR 50' OBJ.
7340	0	0	453	757	529	868	616	995	464	768	540	879	627	1006	481	785	555	894	644	1023
	17	15	283	521	330	595	387	683	290	528	337	602	398	688	301	539	347	612	402	698
	34	30	157	427	183	383	214	426	161	431	187	377	218	430	167	437	192	382	223	435
	51	45	64	168	84	190	86	214	65	169	76	192	88	216	67	171	78	194	90	218
8100	0	0	590	980	666	1078	753	1190	601	991	677	1089	764	1199	618	1008	694	1103	781	1216
	17	15	369	678	431	761	499	853	376	685	439	769	506	860	386	695	449	779	517	817
	34	30	204	432	240	489	296	567	207	435	244	493	301	572	213	441	250	499	305	578
	51	45	83	230	108	275	139	328	85	232	110	277	142	331	87	234	112	279	145	334

NOTE: INCREASE CHART DISTANCES AS FOLLOWS: 75°F + 10%, 100°F + 20%, 125°F + 30%, 150°F + 40%.
OPTIMUM TAKE-OFF WITH ___ RPM, ___ IN.HG. & ___ DEG. FLAP IS 80% OF CHART VALUES.

POWER PLANT SETTINGS (DETAILS ON FIG. ___, SECTION ___)
DATA AS OF ___ BASED ON ___

CLIMB DATA

GROSS WEIGHT LB.	AT SEA LEVEL					AT 5000 FEET					AT 10,000 FEET					AT 15,000 FEET					AT 20,000 FEET					AT 25,000 FEET				
	BEST I.A.S.		RATE OF CLIMB F.P.M.	GAL. OF FUEL USED		BEST I.A.S.		RATE OF CLIMB F.P.M.	FROM SEA LEVEL		BEST I.A.S.		RATE OF CLIMB F.P.M.	FROM SEA LEVEL		BEST I.A.S.		RATE OF CLIMB F.P.M.	FROM SEA LEVEL		BEST I.A.S.		RATE OF CLIMB F.P.M.	FROM SEA LEVEL		BEST I.A.S.		RATE OF CLIMB F.P.M.	FROM SEA LEVEL	
	MPH	KTS				MPH	KTS		TIME MIN.	FUEL USED	MPH	KTS		TIME MIN.	FUEL USED	MPH	KTS		TIME MIN.	FUEL USED	MPH	KTS		TIME MIN.	FUEL USED	MPH	KTS		TIME MIN.	FUEL USED
7340	144	125	3250	7.0		144	125	2860	2.4	13	144	125	2375	4.3	17.2	144	125	1943	6.7	22	144	125	1625	9.5	27.4	144	125	977	13.5	34

OVERLOAD FIGHTER INFORMATION NOT AVAILABLE

FUEL USED (U.S. GAL.) INCLUDES WARM-UP & TAKE-OFF ALLOWANCE

LANDING DISTANCE - FEET

GROSS WEIGHT LB.	BEST IAS APPROACH		POWER ON		HARD DRY SURFACE						FIRM DRY SOD						WET OR SLIPPERY					
	POWER OFF				AT SEA LEVEL		AT 3000 FEET		AT 6000 FEET		AT SEA LEVEL		AT 3000 FEET		AT 6000 FEET		AT SEA LEVEL		AT 3000 FEET		AT 6000 FEET	
	MPH	KTS	MPH	KTS	GROUND ROLL	TO CLEAR 50' OBJ.	GROUND ROLL	TO CLEAR 50' OBJ.	GROUND ROLL	TO CLEAR 50' OBJ.	GROUND ROLL	TO CLEAR 50' OBJ.	GROUND ROLL	TO CLEAR 50' OBJ.	GROUND ROLL	TO CLEAR 50' OBJ.	GROUND ROLL	TO CLEAR 50' OBJ.	GROUND ROLL	TO CLEAR 50' OBJ.	GROUND ROLL	TO CLEAR 50' OBJ.
6075	81	70			794	1355	866	1451	951	1560	875	1436	955	1540	1050	1659	1870	2431	2030	2615	2230	2839
7360	83.5	72.5			835	1390	912	1496	1001	1577	921	1476	1010	1594	1109	1685	1946	2501	2035	2619	2350	2926

DATA AS OF ___ BASED ON ___

REMARKS: TAKE-OFF & LANDING DISTANCES ARE CALCULATED VALUES.

NOTE: TO DETERMINE FUEL CONSUMPTION IN BRITISH IMPERIAL GALLONS, MULTIPLY BY 10, THEN DIVIDE BY 12.

OPTIMUM LANDING IS 80% OF CHART VALUES.

LEGEND
I.A.S.: INDICATED AIRSPEED
M.P.H.: MILES PER HOUR
KTS.: KNOTS
F.P.M.: FEET PER MINUTE

Figure 38—Take-Off, Climb and Landing Chart

Appendix I of this publication shall not be carried in aircraft on combat missions or when there is reasonable chance of its falling into the hands of the enemy.

RESTRICTED

Appendix I

RESTRICTED
AN 01-190FB-1

FLIGHT OPERATION INSTRUCTION CHART

AIRCRAFT MODEL					
FM-2					
ENGINE: R-1820-56					

LIMITS	RPM	M.P. In.Hg.	BLOWER POSITION	MIXTURE POSITION	TIME LIMIT	CYL. TEMP.	TOTAL G.P.H.
WAR EMERG.							
MILITARY POWER	2600	46.5	Low	Auto Lean	30 Min.		147

CHART WEIGHT LIMITS: 7340 TO 7340 POUNDS

EXTERNAL LOAD ITEMS: NONE

NUMBER OF ENGINES OPERATING:

INSTRUCTIONS FOR USING CHART: SELECT FIGURE IN FUEL COLUMN EQUAL TO OR LESS THAN AMOUNT OF FUEL TO BE USED FOR CRUISING. MOVE HORIZONTALLY TO RIGHT OR LEFT AND SELECT RANGE VALUE EQUAL TO OR GREATER THAN THE STATUTE OR NAUTICAL AIR MILES TO BE FLOWN. VERTICALLY BELOW AND OPPOSITE VALUE NEAREST DESIRED CRUISING ALTITUDE (ALT.) READ RPM, MANIFOLD PRESSURE (M.P.) AND MIXTURE SETTING REQUIRED.

NOTES: COLUMN I IS FOR EMERGENCY HIGH SPEED CRUISING ONLY. COLUMNS II, III, IV AND V GIVE PROGRESSIVE INCREASE IN RANGE AT A SACRIFICE IN SPEED. AIR MILES PER GALLON (MI./GAL.) (NO WIND), GALLONS PER HR. (G.P.H.) AND TRUE AIRSPEED (T.A.S.) ARE APPROXIMATE VALUES FOR REFERENCE. RANGE VALUES ARE FOR AN AVERAGE AIRPLANE FLYING ALONE (NO WIND). TO OBTAIN BRITISH IMPERIAL GAL. (OR G.P.H.) MULTIPLY U.S. GAL. (OR G.P.H.) BY 10 THEN DIVIDE BY 12.

COLUMN I (3.13 NAUT.) MI./GAL.

RANGE IN AIRMILES		FUEL U.S. GAL.	RANGE IN AIRMILES	
STATUTE	NAUTICAL		STATUTE	NAUTICAL
510	443	100	360	313
460	399	90	324	282
407	354	80	288	250
357	310	70	252	219
306	266	60	216	188
255	222	50	180	157
204	177	40	144	125
153	133	30	108	94
102	88	20	72	62
51	44	10	36	31

MAXIMUM CONTINUOUS

R.P.M.	M.P. INCHES	MIX-TURE	APPROX. TOT. GPH	T.A.S. MPH	KTS	PRESS ALT. FEET
2500	38	A.L.	58	295	257	40000
2500	38	A.L.	84	314	273	35000
2500	38	A.L.	105	322	280	30000
2500	38	A.L.	100	307	265	25000
2500	43	A.L.	110	304	264	20000
2500	43	A.L.	130	302	262	15000
2500	43	A.L.	129	282	245	10000
						5000
						S.L.

COLUMN II (3.13 NAUT.) MI./GAL.

R.P.M.	M.P. INCHES	MIX-TURE	APPROX. TOT. GPH	T.A.S. MPH	KTS
2500	38	A.L.			
2330	33	A.L.			
2300	31.5	A.L.			
2210	31.4	A.L.			
2240	32.3	A.L.			
2260	33.0	A.L.			

COLUMN III (3.6 STAT. (3.13 NAUT.) MI./GAL.)

STATUTE	NAUTICAL			R.P.M.	M.P. INCHES	MIX-TURE	APPROX. TOT. GPH	T.A.S. MPH	KTS
450	391			2260	32.0	A.L.	86	310	269
405	352			2200	30.0	A.L.	85	307	267
				2150	30.5	A.L.	80	288	250
360	313								
315	274								
270	235								
225	196			2100	29.0	A.L.	79	285	248
180	156			2140	29.0	A.L.	74	268	233
135	117			2160	30.6	A.L.	69	250	217
90	78								
45	39								

COLUMN IV (4.5 STAT. (3.91 NAUT.) MI./GAL.)

STATUTE	NAUTICAL		R.P.M.	M.P. INCHES	MIX-TURE	APPROX. TOT. GPH	T.A.S. MPH	KTS
SUBTRACT FUEL ALLOWANCES NOT AVAILABLE FOR CRUISING								
550	478							
495	430							
440	382							
385	334							
330	286							
275	239		2150	30.3	A.L.	67.0	302	262
220	191		1920	29.0	A.L.	65.0	292	254
165	143		2020	29.0	A.L.	61.6	277	241
110	96							
55	48							
			1850	29.0	A.L.	61.0	274	238
			1800	29.0	A.L.	56.8	255	222
			1850	29.0	A.L.	53	238	207

COLUMN V (5.5 STAT. (4.78 NAUT.) MI./GAL.)

STATUTE	NAUTICAL	FUEL U.S. GAL.	R.P.M.	M.P. INCHES	MIX-TURE	APPROX. TOT. GPH	T.A.S. MPH	KTS	PRESS ALT. FEET
650	565	100							40000
585	508	90							35000
520	452	80							30000
455	395	70							
390	339	60							
325	282	50							
260	226	40							
195	170	30							
130	113	20							
65	56.5	10							

MAXIMUM AIR RANGE

R.P.M.	M.P. INCHES	MIX-TURE	APPROX. TOT. GPH	T.A.S. MPH	KTS
2000	29.0	A.L.	35	227	197
2000	29.0	A.L.	40.7	265	230
1800	29.0	A.L.	39.3	255	222
1620	29.0	A.L.	38	246	214
1600	29.0	A.L.	34.2	222	193
1400	29.0	A.L.	32.0	208	181
1450	29.0	A.L.	30.0	195	170

SPECIAL NOTES

(1) MAKE ALLOWANCE FOR WARM-UP, TAKE-OFF & CLIMB (SEE FIG.) PLUS ALLOWANCE FOR WIND, RESERVE AND COMBAT AS REQUIRED.

EXAMPLE

AT 7340 LB. GROSS WEIGHT WITH 90 GAL. OF FUEL (AFTER DEDUCTING TOTAL ALLOWANCES OF 17 GAL.) TO FLY 324 STAT. AIRMILES AT 5000 FT. ALTITUDE MAINTAIN 2240 RPM AND 32.3 IN. MANIFOLD PRESSURE WITH MIXTURE SET A.L.

LEGEND

ALT.	PRESSURE ALTITUDE
M.P.	MANIFOLD PRESSURE
GPH	U.S. GAL. PER HOUR
TAS	TRUE AIRSPEED
KTS	KNOTS
S.L.	SEA LEVEL

F.R.	FULL RICH
A.R.	AUTO-RICH
A.L.	AUTO-LEAN
C.L.	CRUISING LEAN
M.L.	MANUAL LEAN
F.T.	FULL THROTTLE

RED FIGURES ARE PRELIMINARY DATA, SUBJECT TO REVISION AFTER FLIGHT CHECK

DATA AS OF 1-15-44   BASED ON: Patuxent River Report, Project TED No. PTR-2119

Figure 39 Flight Operation Instruction Chart, Sheet 1 of 2

Appendix I of this publication shall not be carried in aircraft on combat missions or when there is reasonable chance of its falling into the hands of the enemy.

Figure 39 — Flight Operation Instruction Chart, Sheet 2 of 2

Appendix 1

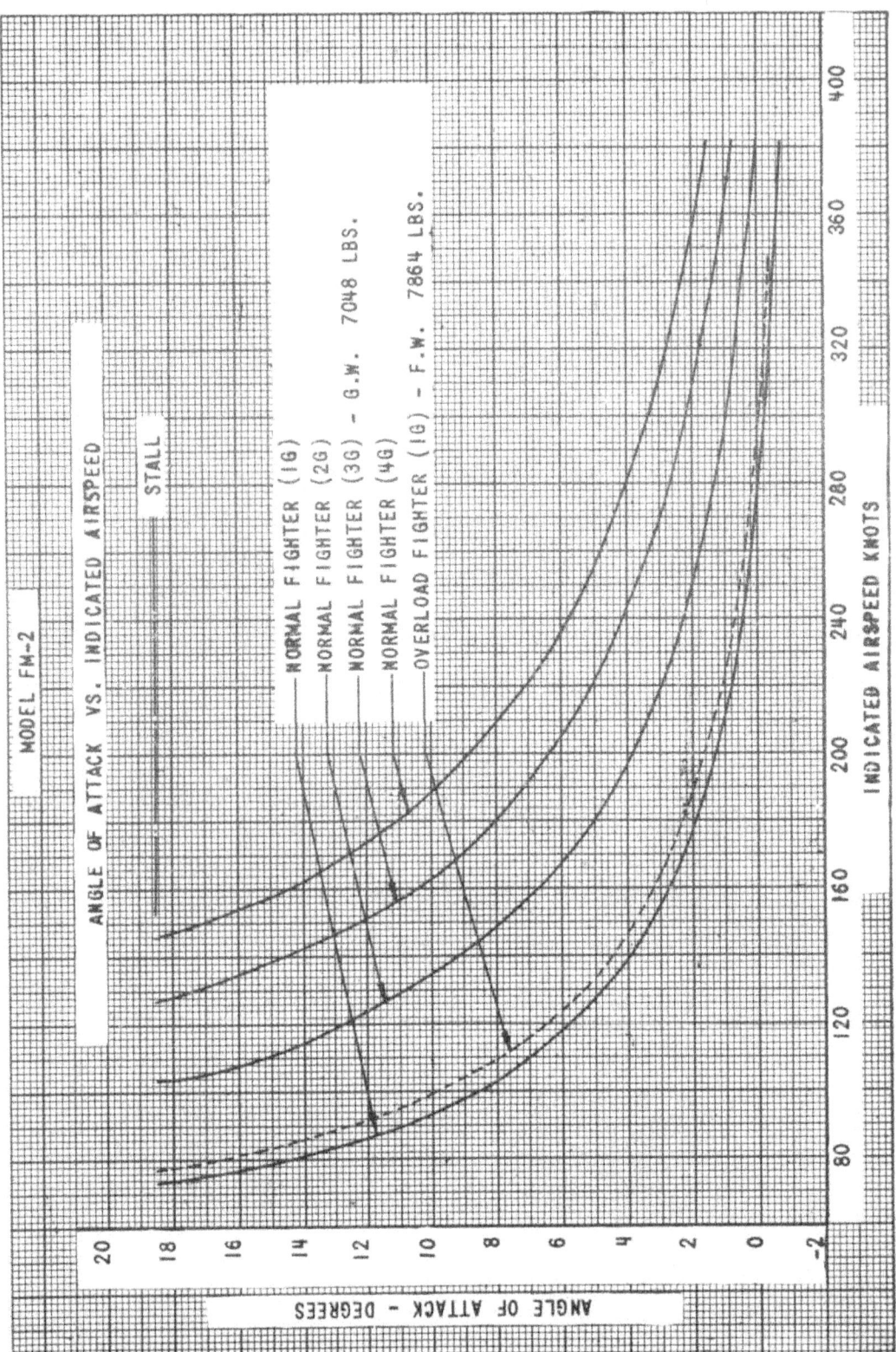

Figure 40 — Angle of Attack vs. Indicated Airspeed Curve

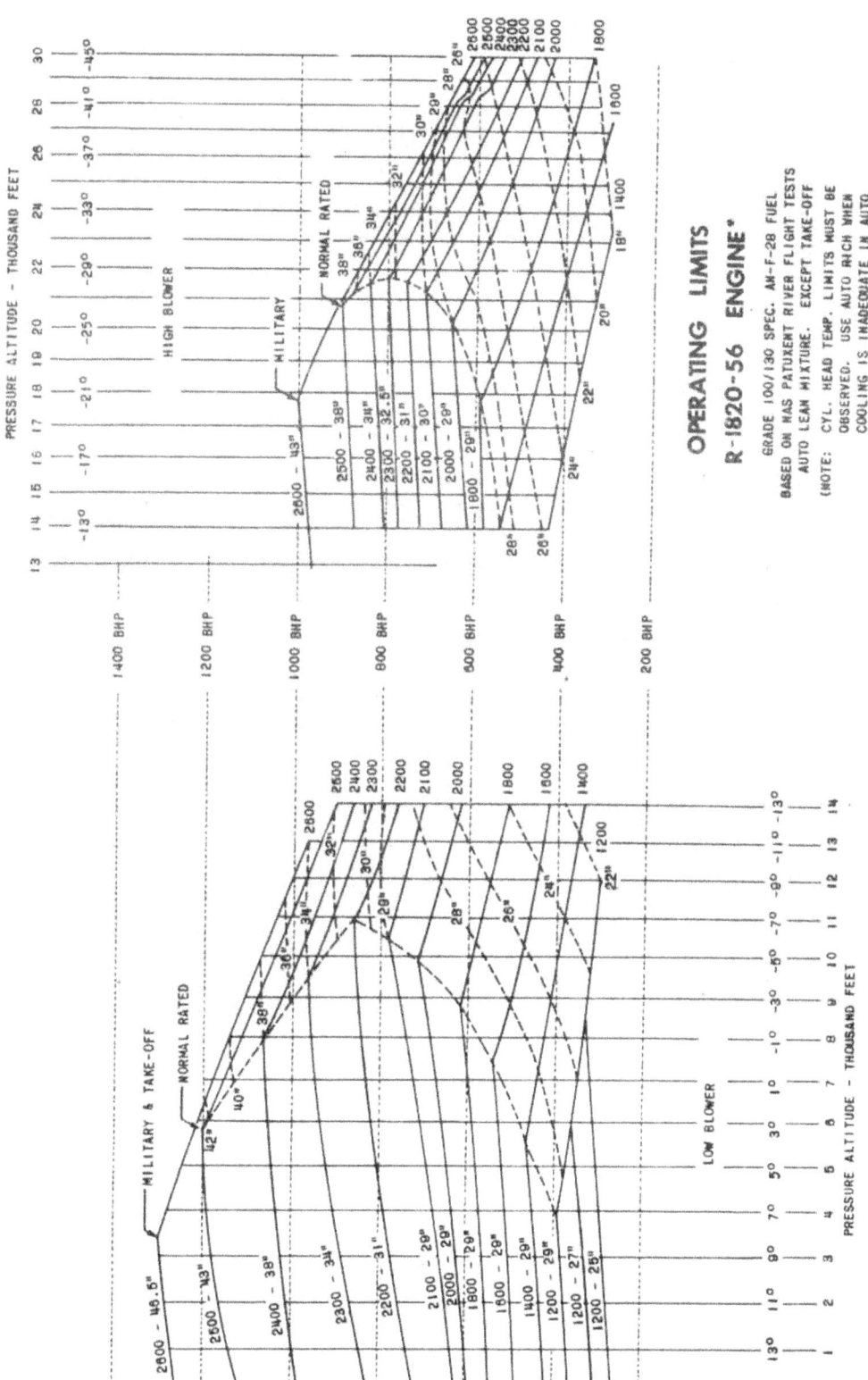

Figure 41—Engine Calibration Curve

Aircraft At War DVD Series

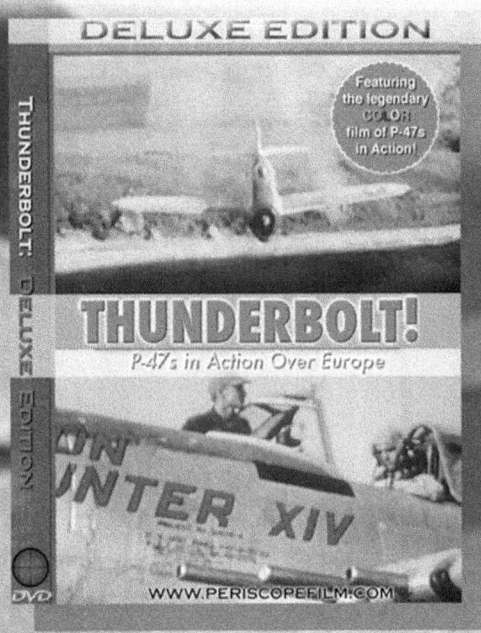
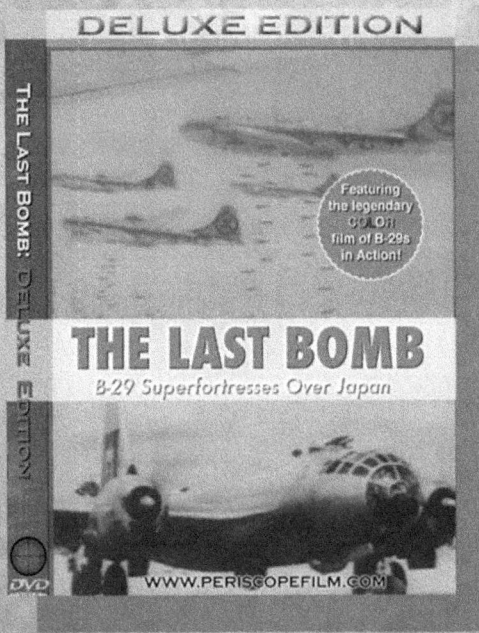
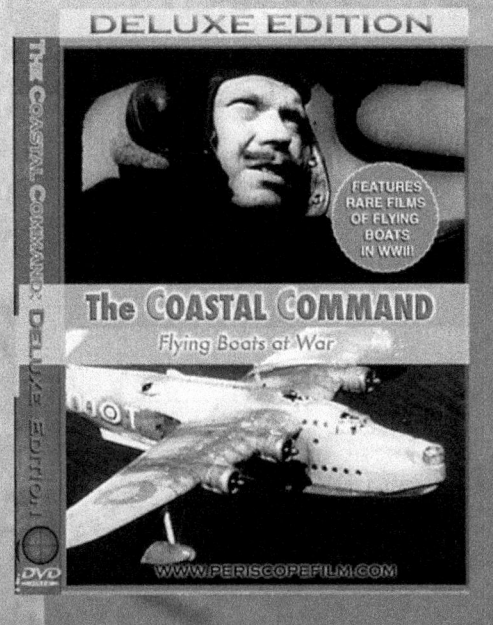

Now Available!

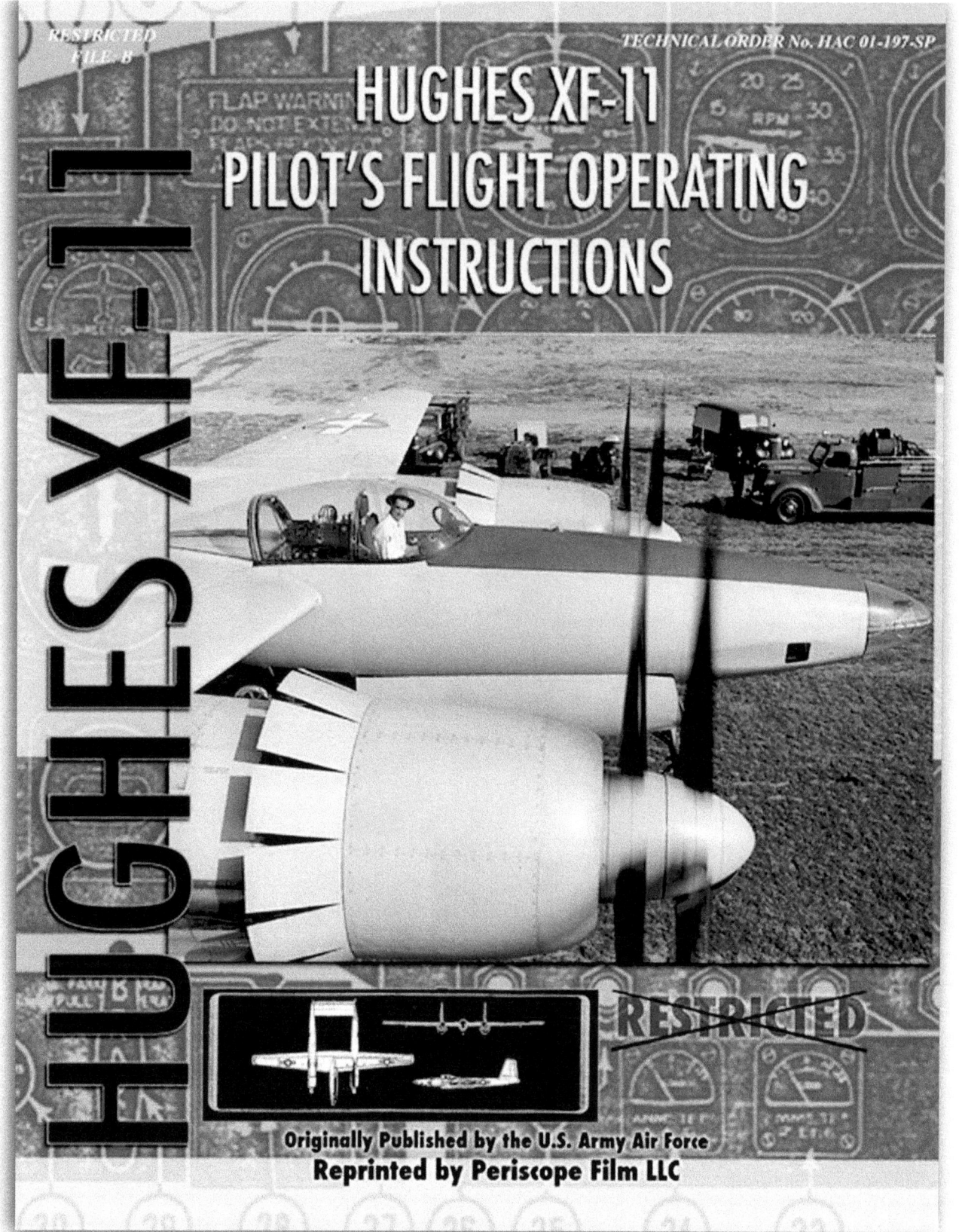

NOW AVAILABLE!

HUGHES FLYING BOAT MANUAL

SPRUCE GOOSE

RESTRICTED

Originally Published by the War Department
Reprinted by Periscope Film LLC

NOW AVAILABLE!

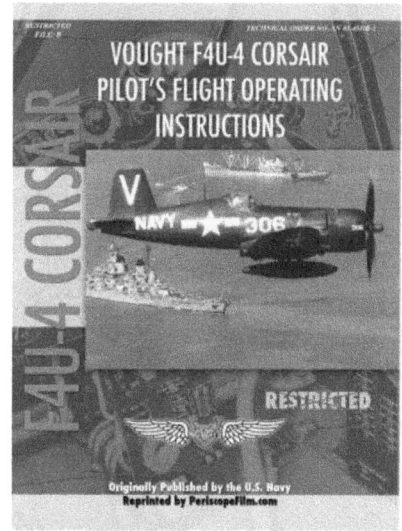
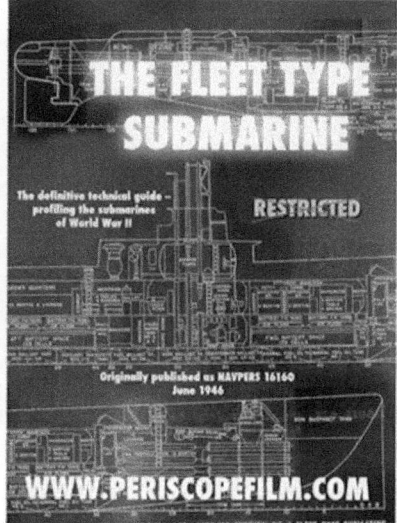

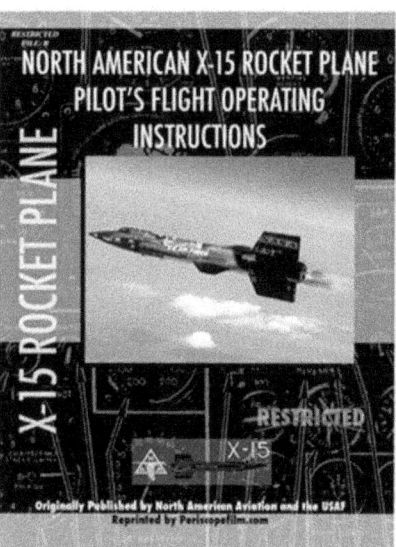
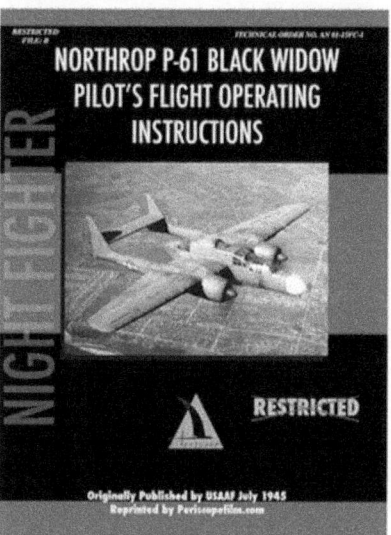

ALSO NOW AVAILABLE FROM PERISCOPEFILM.COM

©2006-2010 Periscope Film LLC
All Rights Reserved
ISBN #978-1-935327-98-1
www.PeriscopeFilm.com

www.ingramcontent.com/pod-product-compliance
Ingram Content Group UK Ltd.
Pitfield, Milton Keynes, MK11 3LW, UK
UKHW051315031225
9359UKWH00032B/680